Encyclopaedic Survey Of

Commonwealth Games

Encyclopaedic Survey Of
Commonwealth Games

Vol. III

A LOOK AT
2010 COMMONWEALTH GAMES

By

Laxman Singh

CYBER TECH PUBLICATIONS
4264/3, Ansari Road, Daryaganj, New Delhi-110002 (India)
Ph.: 011-23244078, 011-43559448 Fax: 011-23280028
E-Mail: cyberpublicationsdelhi@yahoo.com
Website: www.cybertechpublications.com

Encyclopaedic Survey of Commonwealth Games
(Set of 3 Vols.)
Laxman Singh

First Edition 2011

Published by G.S. Rawat
For Cyber Tech Publications
4264/3, Ansari Road, Daryaganj, New Delhi-110002
Ph.: 011-23244078, 011-43559448 Fax: 011-23280028
E-Mail: cyberpublicationsdelhi@yahoo.com
E.mail: cybertechpublications@g.mail.com
website: www.cybertechpublications.com

Printed at: Asian Offset Printers, Delhi-53

Contents

Preface

> "Most controversies would seen be ended, if those engaged in them would first accurately define their terms, and then adhere to their definitions.."
>
> —*Tyron Edwards*

Sports and games competitions are not merely game events, they bring together the participatns from different locales, thus enhancing mutual understanding, universal brotherhood and peace. They have been instrumental in shaping a new world order—in diplomatic as well as economic terms.

Commonwealth Games are the third largest multi-sport event in the world after Summer Olympic Games and the Asian Games.

It is remarkable to note that event was first held in 1930 under the title of the British Empire Games. The event was renamed as the British Empire and Commonwealth Games in 1954, the British Commonwealth Games in 1970, and gained its current title in 1978. Only six teams have attended every Commonwealth Games: Australia, Canada, England, New Zealand, Scotland and Wales. Australia has been the highest scoring team for ten games, England for seven and Canada for one.

The present work encyclopaedic in nature, is an humble attempt to collate vital information on Commonwealth Games.

Judiciously selected information is gathered under the following three volumes:

- Commonwealth Games: Peeping Through History
- Commonwealth Games: Glimpses of Host Cities
- A Look At 2010 Commonwealth Games.

This multidisciplinary work will prove useful to academics and professionals in the field.

In fact, the information contained herein is derived from various authoritative sources, e.g. books, reports, articles and websites. Every care is taken to furnish accurate information. Due to inadvertence there may have crept in some inaccuracies, which we shall correct in subsequent edition, if brought to notice.

We owe a deep sense of gratitude to all those scholars and experts whose works are cited or substantially made use of in the present venture. We express our gratefulness to all source materials and their copyright holders. A number of persons have extended all possible help while working on this project. We are grateful to them also.

Finally, we are thankful to our publishers for materialising this work with every care and patience.

—L.S.

1

Commonwealth Games 2010: An Introduction

India is all set to host the XIX edition of the Commonwealth Games. This is the first major hallmark event to be hosted by New Delhi since the 1982 Asian Games (Asiad' 82). Hallmark events have the ability to transform the urban landscape of a city. Can these games bring about a transformation of Delhi's urban landscape, and if it does, will it do so in an egalitarian fashion? It also looks at worldwide experiences from various other hallmark experiences like the Summer Olympics and the Asian Games, and Delhi's experience with hosting the 1982 Asian Games.

As is generally observed, what one finds is that these events are normally not as beneficial to the host community, as made out to be. More important in India's context is that the benefits are normally even less when the host community is a developing nation, as India is. The enormous expenditure on these is going to be spent largely on the development of civic infrastructure, beautification, transport and sports facilities. If spent effectively, the event can be a catalyst in a much-needed urban regeneration of the city. However past experience from the 1982 Asian Games and actions already undertaken in the run up to the 2010 games suggest that the development may be anti-poor, badly planned and ecologically unsound. It is essential that whatever actions are undertaken in the name of the Commonwealth Games, are well thought out.

"See You in Delhi", was the message that the Indian contingent had for the world, during the closing ceremony of the 2006 Melbourne Commonwealth Games. In 2010, India is going to become the second developing nation ever, to host the Commonwealth Games (CWG), the third largest multi sport event in the world. New Delhi, which has earlier played host to the 1982 Asian Games, is preparing itself to amaze the world. The games have the ability to transform the city's urban landscape and at the same time may simply be an extremely expensive "PR" exercise. Considering the Indian contingent spent Rs. 40 crores on getting the message, "See You in Delhi", across at the closing ceremony of the Melbourne games in an 11-minute show, it might end up being just that. The challenge is to ensure that the potential of the games as a catalyst for change is harnessed.

The CWG is going to be the first mega-event hosted by the city since the 1982 Asian Games, a gap of nearly thirty years. Much has changed, and yet much has remained unchanged in this time.

India is preparing to break out on the world scene as an economic superpower, and the games are a step in propelling India on to the world stage. Yet India is still a poor country, ranked 127 out of 177 in the 20 Human Development Index (HDI), and therefore one must question the rationale of spending more than a billion dollars on a sporting event. Is it going to be simply an exercise in nationalism and politician supported patriotism or is it going to have some notable positive effects on the community, and if so what precisely?

Since 2003, when India won the bid to host the games, various agencies and government bodies have been hard at work making plans for the upcoming event. The over arching theme seems to be to make Delhi a "world class" city by 2010. This of course is a task easier said than done in a city of nearly 15 million people, growing at a phenomenal pace, and largely in a haphazard manner. Urban renewal or regeneration has been a theme in many such events in the past and appears an important one in the 2010 games as well.

This is because it gives an opportunity to improve the infrastructure and appearance of the host city, and also gives global media exposure meaning that the image of a city can be transformed in the eyes of viewers. This was certainly true of Barcelona, which successfully rid itself of its traditional manufacturing city image when hosting the 1992 Olympics (Brown and Massey, 2001). Manchester used the 2002 Commonwealth games as a tool to revive East Manchester, formerly an industrial area that had been suffering low growth and degradation7. The urban landscape Delhi too, is set to change dramatically with many infrastructure projects being pushed through in time for 2010.

In Delhi's bid for the games, it states that through the games, the city wishes to, among other things: Stimulate economic growth and development.

Thus two of the professed aims of the games are to improve the welfare of the citizens of the city through improving facilities and promoting investment in the city. The focus area of the games this time is going to be East

Delhi, across the yamuna, where the games village and some of the venues are to be located. Residents of the area are hoping for a similar transformation as the one South Delhi experienced in the run up to the 1982 games. Infrastructure investments have already increased dramatically in the region with a new bridge being built at Wazirabad, the metro phase 2 being constructed, and numerous flyovers and roads in the pipeline. There are indeed ambitious plans afloat ranging from improving street furniture to setting up more power stations before the 2010 deadline. The work ahead of the games can be broadly grouped into the following:

1. New Stadiums and renovation of existing stadiums
2. Games Village.
3. Transport sector.
4. Urban infrastructure like water and electricity.
5. Efforts to make Delhi "world-class".

Originally the plan was to build a completely new athletics stadium, one that would outrival J.N. Stadium. However lack of funds and available land has meant that the organising team has had to rein in its ambitions. Now the plan is to build one large new stadium, an aquatics centre in the Delhi University with five swimming pools, as well as a new TT hall in the Yamuna Sports Complex and new stadiums for Badminton and Squash in the Siri Fort Sports Complex. The project in DU, which is going to give a major boost to sports there, is to have an Olympic-size (50 metres) pool, a diving pool, pool for synchronised swimming, one for water polo and a warm-up pool as well as a gym. The university is also set to be the venue for the Rugby 7's event.The existing stadiums are however going to need extensive renovation before they can match up to the standards of the CWG. As reported in the Indian Express, the work remaining on the existing stadia is extensive. The estimated expenditure, only for renovation work, is over Rs.1250 Crores. Though construction of new stadiums and upgradation of the existing ones is central to the run up to the Games, the CWG is after all a sporting event; it is by no means the only focus area. Delhi is attempting to give itself a major facelift due to the games, and develop a whole portion of the city, East Delhi and the Yamuna riverfront, which until now has been largely neglected.

As Delhi expands rapidly and space runs out, the until now undeveloped Yamuna riverfront, largely inhabited by slum dwellers and vegetable growers, is looking like prime real estate. The banks of the Yamuna are the largest open space left in the city, as well as the largest groundwater recharge zone. The 25 km stretch along the river has 97 sq km of prime land, 7 per cent of Delhi's total area (Sethi, 2005). DDA and other government authorities seem to have big plans for the area, developing the banks as green spaces and commercial areas. The proposals are centered on a "Thames-type Plan", channeling the river and reclaiming the land for other uses.

A first step in the development of the region is the Games Village, a mammoth Rs. 955 crore project being built on a 63.5-hectare site by the DDA, for the 8000 plus athletes and officials expected for the event. The land has already been acquired from UP at a cost of Rs. 19 Crore and the project is in the planning stage (Vishnoi, 2006). The village will of course not be a one off structure, but will need extensive transport links, amenity providers and so on. There are also eight to nine hotels planned for the area, which will in turn give rise to other auxiliary services coming up. The village will be a well-planned site, with facilities for recreation, commercial activities, hospitals, training, shopping and living, all at hand. Interestingly, one proposal for post event usage is to hand over the village to the Delhi University as hostels, as DU is facing a tremendous shortage of hostel space.

This however seems to have run into rough weather with high costs involved and the DDA now seeming to prefer selling the units as mid income housing post games. Housing too is to get a shotin the arm with over 40,000 low-income housing units to be built before the 2010 games. All this means rampant development of an area that is ecologically fragile and not suited for urban development. Already large structures like the Akshardham Temple, the power plants and the Delhi Secretariat encroach on the riverbed. It is thought to be unadvisable to construct on the riverbed as the area is low-lying and has sandy alluvial soil. Also the region is the city's largest groundwater recharge zone and rampant construction in the area would hamper this considerably. An integral part of the longterm plan for the river area is the channeling of the Yamuna. Many environmentalists however see this as a recipe for disaster. As Amita Baviskar points out "the Yamuna is neither the Thames nor the Seine. Its distinctive rhythm is harmonised to the Indian subcontinent's seasons. With the bulk of its flow concentrated in the monsoons, the Yamuna is liable to breach its embankments if denied its present fertile expanse." Recent events in New Orleans point to the dangers involved with constructing levees and embankments to build on low-lying areas. In a move to ready the area for development, "illegal" structures in the area are being demolished. This means that the slums that have spread in the area have to go, regardless of the fact that low-income housing is practically non-existent in the city and the slum dwellers are getting no relocation.

The numbers can only be said to be frightening, in the last three years as many as 300,000 people have been evicted across New Delhi on top of the 280,000 who are being chased away from Yamuna banks. Many people point out the obvious elitism in these moves, with structures like the Delhi Metro Depot, I.T. Park, near Shastri Park and the Akshardham Temple having to face no such problems, all sites which began construction before the Delhi government issued a 'Public Notice for Change of Land Use". (Sethi, 2005) Others like Dunnu Roy also point out that the reason for which these slums are ostensibly being removed, polluting the river, is illogical as these slums do not even receive enough water to be polluting the river.

Further, the hospitality sector is another area that is estimated to grow rapidly in the coming years, with the help of the Commonwealth Games. The games are estimated to result in a large increase in demand for hotel rooms, with one estimate putting the requirement at 30,000 rooms for 2010. DDA is planning on auctioning over 20 sites for hotels, many in the vicinity of the games village. This would not only add about 7500 rooms, but also raise hundreds of crores for DDA. As of now there are only 6,500 rooms available in the star category hotels and about 7,000 rooms in the budget category. Surrounding states are also preparing to cash in with UP planning on having over 5000 rooms ready before 2010.

Remarkably, transport sector has recently been getting a lot of attention in the last few years as the Delhi government has made it one of their aims to develop an effective mass transport system in the city, and solve the massive congestion problem that the city faces. This emphasis is only set to increase with the games arriving soon. The plans are enormous; flyovers, bypasses, broader roads, a larger metro system, an integrated Rail Bus Transport system, a High Capacity Bus system, an electric trolley bus system and a Light Rail Transit system are all in the pipeline. (Roy, 2006)

The transport sector has already been assigned the lion's share of the Tenth Plan outlay, at 23.68% of Rs. 23000 Crore. The transport infrastructure planned to be in place before 2010 is enormous. 25 new flyovers and underpasses are being planned at an estimated cost of Rs. 1650 Crores. These flyovers are to be largely concentrated in East and South Delhi, as well as on the ring roads so to make them signal-free. An underground tunnel road is also in the pipeline, connecting the J.N. stadium with the Games Village. A new bridge over the Yamuna, at wazirabad, is almost in the construction stage, with the plans for the Rs. 464 Crores project ready. The bridge is at the centre of the regeneration plans that the city government has for the Yamuna area. It is to be the city's first hanging bridge and ready in time for the 2010 Games.

The roads of the city are to get a major facelift before the games with many bypasses and broadening projects planned. Roads like the Mehrauli-Mahipalpur Road, Mehrauli-Badarpur Road and interconnecting roads which link up to the airport are to be broadened. Along with this, roads, which interlink the various stadia, and around major tourist attractions are also to be improved at a cost of nearly Rs. 170 Crores. Two bypasses are also planned at a cost of around Rs 30 Crores (Roy, 2006).

Another ambitious project is to develop a third ring road, which will actually encircle Delhi state. This "peripheral expressway" is projected to be 270 km long, with a 136-km Western Peripheral Expressway and a 134-

km Eastern Peripheral Expressway, and will go through large parts of Haryana, UP and Delhi. This will dramatically reduce pressure on Delhi's existing ring roads, as at the moment inter-state traffic has no way of bypassing the city. This project, which was floated nearly a decade ago, has got a new lease of life with the 2010 Games around the corner, and construction is under way. The maintenance of the two ring roads has also, for the first time, been handed over to private companies. The emphasis of the present Rapid Transport system is now on the Metro. The metro, whose presentation before the Commonwealth Games evaluation team made a sizable impression, is at the core of developing an efficient mass transport system in the city with Phase 1 of the metro being fully operational. However more importantly, phase 2, aimed at extending the network much further in the city, is already under construction, and is set to be ready before 2010. This phase is going to require massive investment, over Rs 8000 Crores. (Chatterjee, 2006).

The second phase is going to provide a vital transport link to East Delhi, with a dedicated Games Village station. The metro, which is already beginning to have an impact on the city's congested roads, will be able to make a much larger impact as its network and reach grows. The second phase, originally planned to be ready by 2010-2011 is now going to be operational by 2009, due to the 2010 Games. The new line may even extend up to the airport in time for the Games. Other transport sector improvements slated for 2010 are 98 km of High Capacity Bus system, 32 km of electric trolley bus system, a Light Rail Transit system, 1,000 quality Radio taxis at airports and major railway stations, 200 new AC buses and 100 mini-buses for athletes, managers and officers and 800 deluxe buses for park-and-ride services for spectators.

There are also plans afoot to set up three smaller ISBT's in the city. One of the most important improvements is to be the newly privatized airport.

The impact that the Games has on providing basic amenities to the city is crucial to how the city's citizens will view the games. It may not be the size of the stadiums or the number of flyovers that are built which will decide whether the games find a place in Delhi'ites hearts; it may be relatively less glamorous things like water, electricity, sanitation and solid waste management. In recent years Delhi has been reeling under a severe water and power shortage, and if the Games are able to expedite movement in these sectors, the citizens of Delhi will be the gainers.

Electricity is the main problem. The summer of 2006 saw one of the worst shortages of power in recent history with the government even attempting to clamp down on usage by homes, shops and commercial establishments. The peak power consumption this summer was 3725 MW; during the Commonwealth Games in 2010, consumption is estimated to be over 7000 MW, nearly double of this year's peak. The government has already got two large new power plants in the pipeline, slated to be ready in time for the Games. However even with these in place, total production of power in Delhi will only reach a maximum capacity of 2300 MW, leaving a shortfall of at least 4700 MW. The two new plants, one in Bawana and the other, an extra unit being added to the existing Pragati plant, are both Gas based, and will add 1000MW and 300 MW respectively to Delhi's production capacity. The present production is dependant on four power plants, The Indraprastha power plant, the Raj Ghat power plant, the Gas Turbine plant and Pragati power plant. However with the exception of the Pragati plant, which is only four years old, none of the plants can produce anywhere close to capacity due to outdated and ill maintained equipment. This makes the city heavily dependent on the Northern Grid for power. The Northern Grid is however already over burdened, supplying electricity to numerous northern states including Uttar Pradesh, Uttarakhand, Haryana, Punjab and Rajasthan. This might lead to a situation of FHB (Family Hold Back) as Jug Suraiya humorously points out in his article "Bhago Dilli". "So all the bijli available, little as it might be, will be diverted from unessential consumers such as hospitals, schools, workplaces and private homes and given to foreign visitors. And if all this diverted bijli proves insufficient, extra supplies can be obtained from neighbouring areas like Gujarat, Madhya Pradesh, Tamil Nadu and the Andaman and Nicobar Islands."(Suraiya, 2006).

This, though exaggerated, may be quite an accurate picture of the situation sans 2010. Delhi's "worldclass" city status will be at stake, and to achieve this, it may be necessary to take some radical steps. The Games will have a very direct impact on power consumption, and we must see whether we are willing to pay the price for hosting the games, with others spending some nights in the dark. Water is another problem very fast taking on crisis proportions. The city has one of the highest per capita water supplies in the world, at over 220 liters per person, per day. Yet water shortages are a perennial problem due to lack of accountability and the fact that they lose about 50 percent of available water. (Yadav, 2006).

There is talk of improving water distribution systems before the 2010 games, a much-needed development for the city's citizens. New pipes will be laid in the area of the village to ensure better distribution. Water supply at stadia will also be upgraded along with and a new water treatment plant at the Games village (to treat a million gallons of water per day. Sanitation and sewerage, is also to be upgraded, and a dedicated sewage treatment plant constructed at the village Solid waste management is another area where work has already begun to prepare the city. Waste management has been privatized in 6 of the 12 MCD zones already and 4 of the remaining 6 will also be privatized shortly.

This step should be able to provide better quality, and save MCD money in the process. A large newspaper in the city recently ran a much publicized campaign called, "From Walled City to World City." The city seems to have begun a concerted effort to achieve what is known in the media as "global standards." In this effort there are numerous steps being taken to transform the face of the city, from better street lighting, to sleeker bus shelters to upgrading the airport. This effort is resulting in over Rs. 100 Crore being spent on street furniture and landscaping alone.(Roy, 2006).

This will give the city a much needed facelift in terms of utilities like bus shelters, dust bins, street lighting and park benches. The other major boost to infrastructure is the airport privatisation. In 1982, a new International Departure and Arrival hall had been built. This time, after a stringent bidding process, the government formally privatized the entire airport, with the GMR group winning the bid. The airport is now set for an overdue modernization plan with capacity to treble, from 10 million to 35 million, by 2010.

This is an essential step towards improving connectivity within India and with the rest of the world, and will also play a determining role in the number of tourists who finally come to Delhi for the 2010 Games. The attempts to make Delhi a "world class" city however has a darker side as it also means that a large number of marginalized people are further marginalized as they do not fit into the larger scheme of things. Demolitions of slums in the Yamuna pushta area have become increasingly commonplace with the site for the Games Village being in the vicinity. Over six lakh hawkers may also face evacuation before the games (Afsal, 2005).

Migrant labour, which entered the city in lakhs in 1982, will probably have to face similar deplorable conditions this time around too. They are needed for the ambitious construction projects envisaged but will have to be kept out of sight, as their conditions would not be in sync with that of a world-class city like Delhi. It is extremely important to ensure that these games do not simply give added benefits to those who are already privileged, but also attempt to aid the marginalised, not further worsen their position. The infrastructure developments that the city needs, will mean investments of over a billion dollars, not including the amount being spent on projects like the metro, airport and peripheral expressway. This is more than three times the estimate that the IOA had made in its bid for the games, which was under 300million dollars.

Like any such event, there are a number of agencies involved, at last count over 45. There are however four primary organisations co coordinating the work; namely the Sports Authority of India, the Delhi Development Authority, the Delhi Government and the Commonwealth Games.

Organising Committee

It is pertinent to note that Delhi government has

asked for Rs 1,314 crore for creating infrastructure, flyovers, new roads and to find a solution to Delhi's chaotic traffic. DDA has to build the athletes' village and the new stadiums at Siri Fort Sports complex and the Yamuna sports complex, and have asked for Rs.983 crore. The Sports Authority of India (SAI) has asked for the biggest chunk of Rs 1,700 crore to renovate all existing stadiums as they are in a bad shape and need an urgent makeover. SAI also needs to build a few more stadiums. The organising committee, which has asked for Rs.980 crores will be spending Rs 200 crore for conducting the games, Rs100 crore for the opening and closing ceremonies, Rs 100 crore for equipment, Rs 50 crore for the expenses at the games village, Rs 40 crore for the media center, Rs 45 lakh to be paid to each of the 71 countries as part of the training expenses.

One can see that at least on paper; the city is all set to transform itself by the time it plays host to the Commonwealth Games. However it is also necessary to keep one thing in mind, and that is that Delhi is otherwise too a rapidly growing city, a dynamic economy and an integral part of India's growth engine. Delhi is estimated to have a population of approx. 192 lakh people by 2010, compared to 140 lakh in 2001, a growth of nearly 40%. This means that it would be wrong to place the causation of all infrastructure and urban development onto the Commonwealth Games. A large amount of it would probably have taken place anyway, the games just gives it a geographical bias and a deadline. The world over there is a serious re-think taking place among city officials as well as academics about the way to go about these events. Do they do more harm than good is not a question that has been answered conclusively, as many of the benefits derived are intangible ones. However it has yet to be conclusively shown that these events are beneficial as well and it is crucial to examine each event independently, studying its unique characteristics, as well as examine previous events and try and learn from their mistakes.

Delhi's citizens have a right to know about the benefits that such events can have to the city, but need to be informed of the downsides as well. The present plan for the Commonwealth Games may be a recipe for an ecological and financial disaster, or they might finally put the city, and the country, on the world map. They may bring in a new era where electricity and water problems, perennial problems in the city, are no longer an issue or they might increase the burden on an already overloaded system. Popular perception tells us that the Asian Games was an unmitigated success. Closer analysis tells us that it was not so simple. The Commonwealth Games, with some smart marketing, may just follow in those footsteps.

In the next chapter we will give a vivid account of the host city of Commonwealth Gams 2010, i.e. Delhi.

2

Delhi: The Host City

Here in the present chapter we will give a vivid picture of Delhi, the host city of Commonwealth Games 2010. Delhi is the largest metropolis by area and the second-largest metropolis by population in India. It is the eighth largest metropolis in the world by population with more than 12.25 million inhabitants in the territory and with nearly 22.2 million residents in the National Capital Region urban area (which also includes Noida, Gurgaon, Greater Noida, Faridabad and Ghaziabad). The name Delhi is often also used to include some urban areas near the NCT, as well as to refer to New Delhi, the capital of India, which lies within the metropolis. The NCT is a federally administered union territory.

Located on the banks of the River Yamuna, Delhi has been continuously inhabited since at least the 6th century BCE. After the rise of the Delhi Sultanate, Delhi emerged as a major political, cultural and commercial city along the trade routes between northwest India and the Gangetic plain. It is the site of many ancient and medieval monuments, archaeological sites and remains. In 1639, Mughal emperor Shahjahan built a new walled city in Delhi which served as the capital of the Mughal Empire from 1649 to 1857.

After the British East India Company had gained control of much of India during the 18th and 19th centuries, Calcutta became the capital both under Company rule and under the British Raj, until George V announced in 1911 that it was to move back to Delhi. A new capital city, New Delhi, was built to the south of the old city during the 1920s. When India gained independence from British rule in 1947, New Delhi was declared its capital and seat of government. As such, New Delhi houses important offices of the federal government, including the Parliament of India, as well as numerous national museums, monuments, and art galleries.

Owing to the migration of people from across the country, Delhi has grown to be a multicultural, cosmopolitan metropolis. Its rapid development and urbanisation, coupled with the relatively high average income of its population, has transformed Delhi. Today, Delhi is a major cultural, political, and commercial centre of India.

Human habitation was probably present in and around Delhi during the second millennium BCE and before, and continuous inhabitation has been evidenced since at least the 6th century BCE. The city is believed to be the site of Indraprastha, legendary capital of the Pandavas in the Indian epic Mahabharata. Settlements grew from the time of the Mauryan Empire (c. 300 BCE).

Remains of seven major cities have been discovered in Delhi. The Tomara dynasty founded the city of Lal Kot in 736 CE. The Chauhan Rajputs of Ajmer conquered Lal Kot in 1180 CE and renamed it Qila Rai Pithora. The Chauhan king Prithviraj III was defeated in 1192 by the Afghan Muhammad Ghori. In 1206, Qutb-ud-din Aybak, the first ruler of the Slave Dynasty established the Delhi Sultanate. Qutb-ud-din started the construction the Qutub Minar and *Quwwat-al-Islam* (might of Islam), the earliest extant mosque in India.

After the fall of the Slave dynasty, a succession of Turkic and Afghan dynasties, the Khilji dynasty, the Tughluq dynasty, the Sayyid dynasty and the Lodhi dynasty held power in the late medieval period, and built a sequence of forts and townships that are part of the seven cities of Delhi. In 1398, Timur Lenk invaded India on the pretext that the Muslim sultans of Delhi were too lenient towards their Hindu subjects. Timur entered Delhi and the city was sacked, destroyed, and left in ruins. Delhi was a major centre of Sufism during the Sultanate period. In 1526, Zahiruddin Babur defeated the last Lodhi sultan in the First Battle of Panipat and founded the Mughal Empire that ruled from Delhi, Agra and Lahore. The Mughal Empire ruled northern India for more than three centuries, with a sixteen-year hiatus during the reign of Sher Shah Suri, from 1540 to 1556.

During 1553–1556, Hemu Vikramaditya acceded to the throne of Delhi by defeating forces of Mughal Emperor Akbar at Agra and Delhi. However, the Mughals reestablished their rule after Akbar's army defeated Hemu during the Second Battle of Panipat. Shah Jahan built the seventh city of Delhi that bears his name (*Shahjahanabad*), and is more commonly known as the *"Old City"* or *"Old Delhi"*.

The old city served as the capital of the Mughal Empire from 1638. After 1680, the Mughal Empire's influence declined rapidly as the Hindu Marathas rose to prominence. A weakened Mughal Empire lost the Battle of Karnal following which the victorious forces of Nader Shah invaded and looted Delhi, carrying away many treasures, including the Peacock Throne. A treaty signed in 1752 made Marathas the protector of the Mughal throne at Delhi. In 1761, after the Marathas lost the third battle of Panipat, Delhi was raided by Ahmed Shah Abdali.

In 1803, the forces of British East India Company overran the Maratha forces near Delhi and ended the Mughal rule over the city. After the Indian Rebellion of 1857, Delhi came under direct rule of the British crown and was made a district province of the Punjab. In 1911, the capital of British India was transferred from Calcutta to Delhi, following which a team of British architects led by Edwin Lutyens designed a new political and administrative area, known as New Delhi, to house the government buildings. New Delhi, also known as *Lutyens' Delhi*, was officially declared as the capital of the Union of India after the country gained independence on 15 August 1947.

During the partition of India, thousands of Hindu and Sikh refugees from West Punjab and Sindh fled to Delhi, while many Muslim residents of the city migrated to Pakistan. Migration to Delhi from the rest of India continues, contributing more to the rise of Delhi's population than the birth rate, which is declining. The Constitution (Sixty-ninth Amendment) Act, 1991 declared the Union Territory of Delhi to be formally known as National Capital Territory of Delhi. The Act gave Delhi its own legislative assembly, though with limited powers. In December 2001, the Parliament of India building in New Delhi was attacked by armed militants resulting in the death of six security personnel. India suspected the hand of Pakistan-based militant groups in the attacks resulting in a major diplomatic crisis between the two countries. Delhi again witnessed terrorist attacks in October 2005 and September 2008 resulting in the deaths of 62 and 30 civilians respectively.

The National Capital Territory of Delhi is spread over an area of 1,484 km^2, of which 783 km^2 is designated rural, and 700 km^2 (270 sq mi) urban. Delhi has a maximum length of 51.9 km nd the maximum width of 48.48 km. There are three local bodies (statutory towns) namely, Municipal Corporation of Delhi (area is 1,397.3 km^2, New Delhi Municipal Committee (42.7 km^2 and Delhi Cantonment Board (43 km^2.

Delhi is an expansive area, in its extremity it spans from Narela in the north to Badarpur in the south. Najafgarh is the furthest point west, and Seemapuri is its eastern extremity. Places like Shahdara and Bhajanpura are its eastern ends and are one of major shopping centres in Delhi.

The NCR encompasses points south and east of the said border, namely Ghaziabad, Noida, Faridabad and Gurgaon. Oddly, the main expanse of Delhi does not follow a specific geographical features (for example, converse to London, which centered on the Thames, has its northern limit at its first Hill, Hampstead Heath, and its southern limit at the river, similarly its western limit is the bottom of a basin – Paddington) The main city area of Delhi does not end until Saket in the South, whilst the northern limit is easily Jahangirpuri, and the western limit is easily Janakpuri-Dwarka. The terrain of Delhi is widely erratic. It changes from plain agricultural fields in the north to dry, arid hills (an offshoot of the Aravalli Hills of Rajasthan) in the south.

There used to be large natural lakes in the southern part of the city, but most of them have dried up due to mining. The city is bordered by river Yamuna, that separates the, although there is a good connectivity between them, with a number of bridges and the Metro subway, areas east of the river. The majority of the city, including New Delhi, lies west of the river. Delhi is located at 28°372 N 77°142 Eÿþ / ÿþ28.61°N 77.23°Eÿþ / 28.61; 77.23, and lies in northern India. It borders the Indian states of Uttar Pradesh on East and Haryana on West, North and South. Delhi lies almost entirely in the Gangetic plains. Two prominent features of the geography of Delhi are the Yamuna flood plain and the Delhi ridge.

The low-lying Yamuna flood plains provide fertile alluvial soil suitable for agriculture. However, these plains are prone to recurrent floods. Reaching up to a height of 318 m (1,043 ft), the ridge forms the most dominating feature in this region. It originates from the Aravalli Range in the south and encircles the west, northeast and northwest parts of the city. Yamuna, a sacred river in Hinduism, is the only major river flowing through Delhi. Another river called the Hindon River separates Ghaziabad from the eastern part of Delhi. Delhi falls under seismic zone-IV, making it vulnerable to major earthquakes, although earthquakes are not so common in Delhi. Delhi has the third highest tree-cover among cities in India.

Climate

Delhi features an atypical version of a humid subtropical climate, with long very hot summers and brief mild winters. Summers are long and extremely hot, from early April to mid-October, with the monsoon season in between. Beginning of March sees a reversal in the direction of wind, from the north-western direction, to the south-western. These bring the hot waves from Rajasthan, carrying sand and are a characteristic of the Delhi summer. These are called *loo*. The months of March to May see a time of hot prickling heat. Monsoon arrives at the end of June, bringing some respite from the heat, but increasing humidity at the same time. Winter starts in late November and peaks in January and is notorious for its heavy fog. Extreme temperatures range from “0.6 °C (30.9 °F) to 46.7 °C (116.1 °F). The annual mean temperature is 25 °C (77 °F); monthly mean temperatures range from 13 °C to 32 °C (56 °F to 90 °F). The average annual rainfall is approximately 714 mm (28.1 inches), most of which is during the [monsoons in July and August. The average date of the advent of monsoon winds in Delhi is 29 June.

As of July 2007, the National Capital Territory of Delhi comprises nine districts, 27 tehsils, 59 census towns, 165 villages and three statutory towns – the Municipal Corporation of Delhi (MCD); thc New Delhi Municipal Committee (NDMC); and the Delhi Cantonment Board (DCB).

The Delhi metropolitan area lies within the National Capital Territory of Delhi (NCT). The NCT has three local municipal corporations: Municipal Corporation of Delhi (MCD), New Delhi Municipal Council (NDMC) and Delhi Cantonment Board. MCD is one of the largest municipal corporations in the world providing civic amenities to an estimated 13.78 million people. The capital of India, New Delhi, falls under the administration of NDMC. The chairperson of the NDMC is appointed by the Government of India in consultation with the Chief Minister of Delhi.

Delhi has four major satellite cities, which lie outside the National Capital Territory of Delhi. These are Gurgaon and Faridabad (in Haryana), and New Okhla Industrial Development Authority (NOIDA) and Ghaziabad, in Uttar Pradesh. Delhi is divided into nine districts. Each district (division) is headed by a Deputy Commissioner and has three subdivisions. A Subdivision Magistrate heads each subdivision. All Deputy Commissioners report to the Divisional Commissioner.

The District Administration of Delhi is the enforcing department for all kinds of State and Central Government policies and exercises supervisory powers over numerous other functionaries of the Government. The Delhi High Court has jurisdiction over Delhi. Delhi also has lower courts: the Small Causes Court for civil cases, and the Sessions Court for criminal cases. The Delhi Police, headed by the Police Commissioner, is one of the largest metropolitan police forces in the world. Delhi is administratively divided into nine police-zones, which are further subdivided into 95 local police stations.

Earlier known as a special union territory, the National Capital Territory of Delhi has its own Legislative Assembly, Lieutenant Governor, Council of Ministers and Chief Minister. The legislative assembly seats are filled by direct election from territorial constituencies in the NCT. However, the Union Government of India and the Government of National Capital Territory of Delhi jointly administer New Delhi. New Delhi, a city in Delhi, is the seat of both the National Capital Territory of Delhi and the Government of India.

While services like transport and others are taken care of by the Delhi government, services such as the police are directly under the control of the Central Government. The legislative assembly was re-established in 1993 for the first time since 1956, with direct federal rule in the span. In addition, the Municipal Corporation of Delhi (MCD) handles civic administration for the city as part of the Panchayati Raj act. New Delhi, an urban area in Delhi, is the seat of both the State Government of Delhi and the Government of India. The Parliament of India, the

Rashtrapati Bhavan (Presidential Palace) and the Supreme Court of India are located in New Delhi. There are 70 assembly constituencies and seven Lok Sabha constituencies in Delhi.

Delhi was a traditional stronghold of the Indian National Congress, also known as the Congress Party. In the 1990s, the Bharatiya Janata Party (BJP) under the leadership of Madan Lal Khurana came into power; however in 1998, Congress regained power under Sheila Dixit, the incumbent Chief Minister. The Congress retained power in the Legislative Assembly in the 2003 and 2008 elections also.

Economy

With an estimated net State Domestic Product (FY 2007) of Rs. 1,182 billion (US$24.5 billion) in nominal terms and Rs. 3,364 billion (US$69.8 billion) in PPP terms, Delhi is the largest commercial center in northern India. In 2007, Delhi had a per capita income of Rs. 66,728 (US$1,450) at current prices, the third highest in India after Chandigarh and Goa as of 2006-07. The tertiary sector contributes 70.95% of Delhi's gross SDP followed by secondary and primary sectors with 25.2% and 3.85% contribution respectively. Delhi's workforce constitutes 32.82% of the population showing an increase of 52.52% between 1991 and 2001. Delhi's unemployment rate decreased from 12.57% in 1999–2000 to 4.63% in 2003. In December 2004, 636,000 people were registered with various employment exchange programmes in Delhi. In 2001 the total workforce in all government (union and state) and quasi-government sector was 620,000. In comparison, the organised private sector employed 219,000. Key service industries include information technology, telecommunications, hotels, banking, media and tourism. Delhi's manufacturing industry has also grown considerably as many consumer goods industries have established manufacturing units and headquarters in and around Delhi. Delhi's large consumer market, coupled with the easy availability of skilled labour, has attracted foreign investment in Delhi.

In 2001, the manufacturing sector employed 1,440,000 workers while the number of industrial units was 129,000. Construction, power, telecommunications, health and community services, and real estate form integral parts of Delhi's economy. Delhi has India's largest and one of the fastest growing retail industries. As a result, land prices are booming and Delhi is currently ranked the 7th most expensive office hotspot in the world, with prices at $145.16 per square foot. As in the rest of India, the fast growth of retail is expected to affect the traditional unorganized retail trading system.

The water supply in Delhi is managed by the Delhi Jal Board (DJB). As of 2006, it supplied 650 MGD (million gallons per day) of water, while the water demand for 2005–06 was estimated to be 963 MGD. The rest of the demand is met by private and public tube wells and hand pumps. At 240 MGD, the Bhakra storage is the largest water source for DJB, followed by river Yamuna and Ganges. With falling groundwater level and rising population density, Delhi faces severely acute water shortage. Delhi daily produces 8000 tonnes of solid wastes which is dumped at three landfill sites by MCD. The daily domestic waste water production is 470 MGD and industrial waste water is 70 MGD. A large portion of the sewerage flows untreated into the river Yamuna.

The city's per capita electricity consumption is about 1,265 kWh but actual demand is much more. In 1997, Delhi Vidyut Board (DVB) replaced Delhi Electric Supply

Undertaking which was managed by the MCD. The DVB itself cannot generate adequate power to meet the city's demand and borrows power from India's Northern Region Grid. As a result, Delhi faces a power shortage resulting in frequent blackouts and brownouts, especially during the summer season when energy demand is at its peak. Several industrial units in Delhi rely on their own electrical generators to meet their electric demand and for back up during Delhi's frequent and disruptive power cuts. A few years ago, the power sector in Delhi was handed over to private companies. The distribution of electricity is carried out by companies run by Tata Power and Reliance Energy. The Delhi Fire Service runs 43 fire stations that attend about 15,000 fire and rescue calls per year.

State-owned Mahanagar Telephone Nigam Limited (MTNL) and private enterprises like Vodafone Essar, Airtel, Idea cellular, Reliance Infocomm, and Tata Indicom provide telephone and cell phone service to the city. In May 2008, Airtel alone had approximately 4 million cellular subscribers in Delhi. Cellular coverage is extensive, and both GSM and CDMA (from Reliance and Tata Indicom) services are available. Affordable broadband internet penetration is increasing in the city.

Transport

Public transport in Delhi is provided by buses, auto rickshaws and a metro rail system.

Buses are the most popular means of transport catering to about 60% of the total demand. The state-owned Delhi Transport Corporation (DTC) is a major bus service provider for the city. The DTC operates the world's largest fleet of environment-friendly CNG buses. A Bus rapid transit network runs between Ambedkar Nagar and Delhi Gate

The Delhi Metro, a mass rapid transit system built and operated by Delhi Metro Rail Corporation (DMRC), serves many parts of Delhi as well as the satellite city of Noida in neighbouring Uttar Pradesh. As of April 2010, the metro consists of five lines with a total length of 111 km (69 mi) and 98 stations while several other lines are under construction. Line 1 runs between Rithala and Shahdara, Line 2 runs between Jahangirpuri and the Central Secretariat and Line 3 runs between Dwarka Sector 9 and Noida City Centre. Line 4 runs between Yamuna Bank and Ananad Vihar. The fifth line runs from Inderlok to Mundka. Phase-II of the network is under construction and will have a total length of 128 km. It is expected to be completed by 2010. The Phase-I was built at a cost of US$2.3 billion and the Phase-II will cost an additional US$4.3 billion. Phase-III and IV will be completed by 2015 and 2020 respectively, creating a network spanning 413.8 km, longer than that of the London Underground.

Though notorious auto rickshaws are a popular means of public transportation in Delhi, as they charge a lower fare than taxis. Most run on Compressed Natural Gas (CNG) and are yellow and green in colour. Taxis are not an integral part of Delhi public transport, though they are easily available. Private operators operate most taxis, and most neighborhoods have a taxi stand from which taxis can be ordered or picked up. In addition, air-conditioned radio taxis, which can be ordered by calling a central number, have become increasingly popular, charging a flat rate of Rs. 15 per kilometre.

Delhi is a major junction in the rail map of India and is the headquarters of the Northern Railway. The five main railway stations are New Delhi Railway Station, Old Delhi, Nizamuddin Railway Station, Anand Vihar Railway

Terminal and Sarai Rohilla. Delhi is connected to other cities through many highways and expressways. Delhi currently has three expressways and three are under construction to connect it with its prosperous and commercial suburbs. The Delhi-Gurgaon Expressway connects Delhi with Gurgaon and the international airport. The DND Flyway and Noida-Greater Noida Expressway connect Delhi with two prosperous suburbs. Greater Noida is to have the new airport while Noida is to have the Indian Grand Prix.

Indira Gandhi International Airport (DEL) is situated in the western corner of Delhi and serves as the main gateway for the city's domestic and international civilian air traffic. In 2006–07, the airport recorded a traffic of more than 23 million passengers, making it one of the busiest airports in South Asia. A new US$1.93 billion Terminal 3 is currently under construction and will handle an additional 34 million passengers annually by 2010. Further expansion programs will allow the airport to handle more than 100 million passengers per annum by 2020. Safdarjung Airport is the other airfield in Delhi used for general aviation purpose.

Private vehicles account for 30% of the total demand for transport. At 1922.32 km of road length per 100 km^2, Delhi has one of the highest road densities in India. Delhi is well connected to other parts of India by five National Highways: NH 1, 2, 8, 10 and 24. Roads in Delhi are maintained by MCD (Municipal Corporation of Delhi), NDMC, Delhi Cantonment Board, Public Works Department (PWD) and Delhi Development Authority. Delhi's high population growth rate, coupled with high economic growth rate has resulted in an ever increasing demand for transport creating excessive pressure on the city's existent transport infrastructure. As of 2008. Also, the number of vehicles in the metropolitan region, i.e., Delhi NCR is 112 lakhs (11.2 million).

In 2008, there were 85 cars in Delhi for every 1,000 of its residents. In order to meet the transport demand in Delhi, the State and Union government started the construction of a mass rapid transit system, including the Delhi Metro. In 1998, the Supreme Court of India ordered all public transport vehicles to use compressed natural gas (CNG) as fuel instead of diesel and other hydro-carbons.

Many ethnic groups and cultures are represented in Delhi, making it a cosmopolitan city. Being the political and economic hub of northern India, the city attracts workers – both blue collar and white collar – from all parts of India, further enhancing its diverse character. A diplomatic hub, home to the embassies of 160 countries, Delhi has a large expatriate population as well.

According to the 2001 Census of India, the population of Delhi that year was 13,782,976. The corresponding population density was 9,294 persons per km^2, with a sex ratio of 821 women per 1000 men, and a literacy rate of 81.82%. By 2004, the estimated population had increased to 15,279,000. That year, the birth rate, death rate and infant mortality rate (per 1000 population) were 20.03, 5.59 and 13.08, respectively. As of 2007, the National Capital Territory of Delhi had an estimated population of 21.5 million people, making it the second largest metropolitan area in India after Mumbai. According a 1999–2000 estimate, the total number of people living below the poverty line, defined as living on $11 or less per month, in Delhi was 1,149,000 (which was 8.23% of the total population, compared to 27.5% of India as a whole).

In 2001, the population of Delhi increased by 285,000

as a result of migration and by an additional 215,000 as a result of natural population growth – this made Delhi one of the fastest growing cities in the world. By 2015, Delhi is expected to be the third largest agglomeration in the world after Tokyo and Mumbai. Dwarka, Asia's largest planned residential colony, is located within the National Capital Territory of Delhi.

On religious plane, Hinduism is the religion of 82% of Delhi's population. There are also large communities of Muslims (11.7%), Sikhs (4.0%), Jains (1.1%) and Christians (0.9%) in the city. Other minorities include Parsis, Anglo-Indians, Buddhists and Jews.

Hindustani language is the principal spoken language while English is the principal written language of the city. Other languages commonly spoken in the city are dialects of Hindi, Punjabi and Urdu. The linguistic groups from all over India are well represented in the city; among them are Punjabi, Haryanvi, UP, Bihari, Bengali, Sindhi, Tamil, Rajasthani, Garhwali, Telugu, North-East, Kannada, Malayalam, Marathi and Gujarati.

In 2005, Delhi accounted for the highest percentage (16.2%) of the crimes reported in the 35 cities in India with populations of one million or more. The city also has the highest rate of crime against women (27.6 compared to national average rate of 14.1 per 100,000) and against children (6.5 compared to national average of 1.4 per 100,000) in the country.

Culture

Delhi's culture has been influenced by its lengthy history and historic association as the capital of India. This is exemplified by the many monuments of significance found in the city; the Archaeological Survey of India recognises

1200 heritage buildings and 175 monuments in Delhi as national heritage sites. The Old City is the site where the Mughals and the Turkic rulers constructed several architectural marvels like the Jama Masjid and Red Fort. Three World Heritage Sites—the Red Fort, Qutab Minar and Humayun's Tomb—are located in Delhi. Other monuments include the India Gate, the Jantar Mantar (an 18th century astronomical observatory) and the Purana Qila (a 16th century fortress). The Laxminarayan Temple, Akshardham and the Bahá'í Lotus Temple are examples of modern architecture. Raj Ghat and associated memorials houses memorials of Mahatma Gandhi and other notable personalities. New Delhi houses several government buildings and official residences reminiscent of the British colonial architecture. Important structures include the Rashtrapati Bhavan, the Secretariat, Rajpath, the Parliament of India and Vijay Chowk. Safdarjung's Tomb is an example of the Mughal gardens style.

Delhi's association and geographic proximity to the capital, New Delhi, has amplified the importance of national events and holidays. National events like Republic Day, Independence Day and *Gandhi Jayanti* (Gandhi's birthday) are celebrated with great enthusiasm in Delhi. On India's Independence Day (15 August) the Prime Minister of India addresses the nation from the Red Fort. Most Delhiites celebrate the day by flying kites, which are considered a symbol of freedom. The Republic Day Parade is a large cultural and military parade showcasing India's cultural diversity and military might. Over the centuries Delhi is known for its composite culture, and a festival that symbolizes it truly is the Phool Walon Ki Sair, which takes place each year in September, and where flowers and fans embroidered with flowers, *pankha* are offered to the shrine of 13th century Sufi saint, Khwaja Bakhtiyar Kaki, along with the Yogmaya Temple also situated in Mehrauli. Religious festivals include Diwali (the festival of lights), Mahavir Jayanti, Guru Nanak's Birthday, Durga Puja, Holi, Lohri, Maha Shivaratri, Eid ul-Fitr and Buddha Jayanti. The Qutub Festival is a cultural event during which performances of musicians and dancers from all over India are showcased at night, with the Qutub Minar as the chosen backdrop of the event. Other events such as Kite Flying Festival, International Mango Festival and *Vasant Panchami* are held every year in Delhi. The Auto Expo, Asia's largest auto show, is held in Delhi biennially.

The World Book Fair, held biannually at the Pragati Maidan, is the second largest exhibition of books in the world with as many as 23 nations participating in the event. Delhi is often regarded as the "Book Capital" of India because of high readership.

Home to different cuisine, Punjabi and Mughlai delicacies like kababs and biryanis are popular in Delhi. Due to Delhi's large cosmopolitan and migrant population, cuisines from every part of India, including Gujarati Rajasthani, Maharashtrian, Bengali, Hyderabadi cuisines, and South Indian food items like idli, sambar and dosa are widely available. Local delicacies include *Chaat* and *Dahi-Papri*. There are several food outlets in Delhi serving international cuisine, including Italian, Japanese, and Chinese. Within the last decade western fast food has become more popular as well.

Historically, Delhi has always remained an important trading centre in northern India. Old Delhi still contains legacies of its rich Mughal past, which can be found among the old city's tangle of snaking lanes and teeming bazaars. The dingy markets of the Old City have an eclectic product range, from oil-swamped mango, lime and eggplant pickles, candy-colored herbal potions to silver jewelry, bridal attire, uncut material and linen, spices, sweets. Some of old regal *havelis* (palatial residences) are still there in the Old City. Chandni Chowk, a three-century-old shopping area, is one of the most popular shopping areas in Delhi for jewellery and *Zari* saris.

Notable among Delhi's arts and crafts are the *Zardozi* (an embroidery done with gold thread) and *Meenakari* (the art of enameling). Dilli Haat, Hauz Khas, Pragati Maidan offer a variety of Indian handicrafts and handlooms. Over time Delhi has absorbed a multitude of humanity from across the country and has morphed into an amorphous pool of cultural styles.

Education

Schools and higher educational institutions in Delhi are administered either by the Directorate of Education, the NCT government, or private organizations. In 2004–05, there were 2,515 primary, 635 middle, 504 secondary and 1,208 senior secondary schools in Delhi. That year, the higher education institutions in the city included 165 colleges, among them five medical colleges and eight engineering colleges, six universities (Delhi University, Jawaharlal Nehru University, Jamia Millia Islamia, Guru Gobind Singh Indraprastha University (GGSIPU), National Law University, Delhi, Indira Gandhi National Open University (IGNOU) and Jamia Hamdard), and nine deemed universities. GGSIPU and National Law University, Delhi are the only state universities; IGNOU is for open/distance learning; the rest are all central universities.

Private schools in Delhi—which employ either English or Hindi as the language of instruction—are affiliated to one of two administering bodies: the Council for the Indian

School Certificate Examinations (CISCE), the Central Board for Secondary Education (CBSE) and the National Institute of Open Schooling (NIOS). In 2004–05, approximately 15.29 lakh (1.529 million) students were enrolled in primary schools, 8.22 lakh (0.822 million) in middle schools and 6.69 lakh (0.669 million) in secondary schools across Delhi. Female students represented 49% of the total enrollment. The same year, the Delhi government spent between 1.58% and 1.95% of its gross state domestic product on education.

After completing the ten-year secondary phase of their education under the 10+2+3 plan, students typically spend the next two years either in junior colleges or in schools with *senior secondary* facilities, during which their studies become more focused. They select a *stream* of study—liberal arts, commerce, science, or, less commonly, vocational.

Upon completion, those who choose to continue, either study for a three-year undergraduate degree at a college, or a professional degree in law, engineering, or medicine. Notable higher education or research institutes in Delhi include All India Institute of Medical Sciences, Dr.Ram Manohar Lohia Hospital & PGIMER, Jawaharlal Nehru University, Indian Institute of Technology Delhi, Delhi Technological University, Indian Law Institute, Delhi School of Economics, Jamia Millia Islamia and Indian Institute of Foreign Trade. As of 2008, about 16% of all Delhi residents possessed at least a college graduate degree.

Media

As the capital of India, New Delhi is the focus of political reportage, including regular television broadcasts of Parliament sessions. Many country-wide media agencies, among them the state-owned Press Trust of India and Doordarshan, are based in the city. Television programming in the city includes two free terrestrial television channels offered by Doordarshan, and several Hindi, English and *regional-languages* cable channels offered by multi system operators. Satellite television, in contrast, has yet to gain large-scale subscribership in the city.

A hub of journalism, print journalism remains a popular news medium in Delhi. During 2004–05, 1029 newspapers in thirteen languages were published from the city. Of these, 492 were Hindi language newspapers, including *Navbharat Times*, *Hindustan Dainik*, *Punjab Kesari*, *Dainik Jagran*, *Dainik Bhaskar* and *Dainik Desbandhu*. Amongst the English language newspapers, *The Hindustan Times*, with over a million copies in circulation, was the single largest daily. Other major English newspapers include *Times of India*, *The Hindu*, *Indian Express*, *Business Standard*, *The Pioneer* and *Asian Age*. Regional dailies include *Malayala Manorama* and *Dinakaran*.

Radio is a less popular mass medium in Delhi, although FM radio has been gaining ground since the inauguration of several new FM channels in 2006. A number of state-owned and private radio stations broadcast from Delhi, including All India Radio (AIR), one of the world's largest radio service providers, which offers six radio channels in ten languages. Other city-based radio stations include "Aaj Tak", "Radio City(91.1 MHz)", "Big FM(92.7 MHz)", "Red FM(93.5MHz)", "Radio One(94.3 MHz)", "Hit FM(95 MHz)", "Apna Radio", "Radio Mirchi(98.3 MHz)", "FM Rainbow(102.4 MHz)", "Fever FM(104 MHz)", "Meow FM(104.8 MHz)", "FM Gold(106.4 MHz)".

Sports

Cricket is the most popular sport in Delhi. There are several cricket grounds (or *maidans*) located across the city. The Feroz Shah Kotla stadium is one of the oldest cricket grounds in India and is a venue for international cricket matches. The Delhi cricket team represents the city in the Ranji Trophy, a domestic first-class cricket championship. The city is also home to the IPL team Delhi Daredevils, and ICL team Delhi Giants (earlier named Delhi Jets). Other sports such as field hockey, football (soccer), basketball, tennis, golf, badminton, swimming, kart racing, weightlifting and table tennis are also popular in the city.

Jawaharlal Nehru Stadium and the Indira Gandhi Indoor Stadium are other stadiums in Delhi. In the past, Delhi has hosted several domestic and international sporting events, such as the First and the Ninth Asian Games. Delhi is preparing itself to host the 2010 Commonwealth Games, projected to be the largest multi-sport event ever held in the city. Delhi lost bidding for the 2014 Asian Games, and considered making a bid for the 2020 Summer Olympics.

REFERENCES

Aitken, Bill (2001) [2002]. *Speaking Stones: World Cultural Heritage Sites in India*. Eicher Goodearth Limited.

Asher, Catherine B (2000) [2000]. "Chapter 9:Delhi walled: Changing Boundaries". in James D. Tracy. *City Walls*. Cambridge University Press. pp. 247–281.

Austin, Ian; Thhakur Nahar Singh Jasol. "Chauhans (Cahamanas, Cauhans)". *The Mewar Encyclopedia*.

Bakshi, S.R. (1995) [2002]. *Delhi Through Ages*. Anmol Publications Pvt. Ltd. p. 2.

Cohen, Richard J. (October–December 1989). "An Early Attestation of the Toponym Dhilli". *Journal of the American Oriental Society* 109 (4): 513–519.

"GIS-Based Spatial Information Integration, Modeling and Digital

Mapping: A New Blend of Tool for Geospatial Environmental Health Analysis for Delhi Ridge" (PDF).

Mayaram, Shail. *Against history, against state: counterperspectives from the margins,* Cultures of history. Columbia University Press, 2003.

Necipoglu, Gulru (2002) [2002]. "Epigraphs, Scripture, and Architecture in the Early Sultanate of Delhi". *Muqarnas: An Annual on the Visual Culture of the Islamic World.* BRILL. pp. 12–43.

"Provisional Population Totals: Delhi". *Provisional Population Totals : India . Census of India 2001, Paper 1 of 2001.*

Sehgal, R.L. (1998) [1998]. *Slum Upgradation: Emerging Issue & Policy Implication's.* Bookwell Publications. p. 97.

Smith, George (1882). *The Geography of British India, Political & Physical.* J. Murray. pp. 216–217.

Upadhyay, R (16 February 2004). "Sufism in India: Its Origin, History and Politics". South Asia Analysis Group.

3

Commonwealth Games 2010 and Urban Development

From October 2010 onward New Delhi will play host to the third largest multi-sporting event in the world, with tens of thousands of visitors descending upon the city. To prepare itself for this, the city is planning a major overhaul of its urban infrastructure as well as its sporting facilities. These events happen in a city once in a decade or maybe even less, (the last large event held in Delhi was the 1982) and have the ability to transform it. Sports is now a very passionate and among many, an obsessive subject. In the run up to the Football World Cup 2006, the theme of football as a unifying religion has been played up numerous times in the media. Academicians even postulate that „religious pilgrimages of the past have been replaced by modern pilgrimages to such spectacles as the Olympic Games, the FIFA World Cup and other such events' (Gibson, 1998). Sporting events have now indeed become "spectacles", and with over 5 billion viewers expected, can give the host community a lot of exposure. India however still remains to make its mark on the world as a sporting nation. With the exception of cricket, and a handful of gifted individuals, Indians have performed quite miserably on the world stage. If one was to examine the last Olympics medal tally by population, that is, population divided by number of medals, India comes last by an enormous margin. Even after the 1982 Asian Games, which gave a dramatic boost to sports facilities in the country, our performance is yet to match international standards.

There are, therefore, some hard questions that need to be answered before one can conclude that such an event has a positive effect on the host community. Is the amount spent on such events worth it? One must remember that the funds that typically go into supporting these events are public funds and therefore should benefit society at large, or at least a large portion, and not just an elite minority. Some other questions that arise out of such events, with particular relevance in this paper, is its impact on the urban scene. Will the event lead to rampant and unchecked development, possibly unplanned? Will the infrastructure created be beneficial post-event or will it remain under utilised and fall into disrepair? Will the city's infrastructure be able to bear the strain of thousands of visitors that flood the city during such an event? Will the event prove to be a hindrance to the city's residents during the event? Will the event actually prove to be a boost to the domestic sports scene? There are numerous questions that arise from such events, many with inconclusive answers. However it is important for a prospective bidder of international sporting events, like New Delhi is, to carefully study all the pros and cons of such an event, and not fall into the trap of making it an issue of "national prestige."

The world over, cities vie with each other to host "hallmark" events such as the Olympics, World Cup's etc. It is seen by many as a sure way of shooting the host city into the limelight, resulting in an "economic windfall" (Baade and Matheson, 2003), and at the same time giving these host cities the impetus to improve domestic facilities and infrastructure. The impact of being the host city, range from the physical (construction projects) to the intangible (local self-esteem or international impact). The impact that an event of this kind has on the urban landscape can largely be gauged by the size of the "legacy" that it creates. It is important to note here that it is not only legacy creation that is important, but creating a legacy which is beneficial to the host community post games, and which justifies the costs involved.

The controversy surrounding these events however is centred on its economic sense. Do these games make money for the host city or not? The data from past Olympic games seems to suggest not. All recent Summer Games with the sole exception of the 1984 Los Angeles Games have lost money. The citizens of Munich continue to pay a special tax to this day, to pay off debt incurred in the 1976 Games (Preuss, 1998). This is very often not revealed to the public by using smart accounting techniques that do not include a lot of the costs incurred under direct games expenditure. After the $200 million profit that L.A. made on the games in '84, they have been increasingly looked upon as extremely profitable, though LA's performance is yet to be replicated (Baade and Matheson 2003). Interestingly only Los Angeles bid for the 1984 Games, largely due to the financial disasters that the Montreal and Moscow Olympic Games in 1976 and 1980 were. This fact explains the absence of significant public sector financial support in Los Angeles, and, perhaps, the private financial success the 1984 Games are thought to have enjoyed. Even here though employment effects and increased economic activity seem to have been transitory.

When numerous bidders are present however,

theoretically the winning bid would be constant with a zero economic return on the investment if opportunity costs were included in the bidding calculus. The political nature of the event has however ensured that the games give a negative return. In other words government is willing to pay something for perceived political gains (Baade and Matheson, 2002).

Today, the bid process has also become a very expensive and long drawn out affair. Some estimates place the amount spent by potential hosts for the 2012 Olympics during the bidding process at nearly 200 million euros.

In more recent years, therefore, hosting sporting events has been viewed as a prestigious achievement resulting in opportunities for economic profit, urban regeneration and global media exposure. Increasingly such sporting events are being aimed at increasing the exposure and visibility of the host city, and many academicians believe that success cannot be simply decided by profit and loss, as there are many intangible and unaccounted for benefits (Brown and Massey, 2001) Urban regeneration and the re-imaging of cities is now a central aspect of game bids. Barcelona and Manchester can be viewed as partially successful in that they were able to re align the popular image of the city, both of which were manufacturing centres to that of tourist destinations as trendy European cities. In Delhi too, the emphasis is on portraying Delhi as a "world class" city, one of "international standards." This is of course a little more problematic in third world conditions as it requires a further marginilisation of the poor to portray this "image" to the world.

In Barcelona, for example, the largest component of investment went into the development of roads and transport facilities, while the construction of offices, commercial property, hotels and sports facilities also made up a large proportion.

The importance of the urban transformation of Barcelona due to the Games is seen in these proportions: in relation to the dimension in 1989, the new road projects meant an increase in expediture of 15%, the new sewerage systems an increase of 17%, new green zones and beaches an increase of 78%, and ponds and fountains, an increase of 268%. (Brunet, 1995). Sporting events of these kinds are increasingly being seen as vehicles for urban renewal, a catalyst to create iobs, increase investment and transform the landscape of the city. The 2002 Commonwealth Games in Manchester were aimed primarily to "regenerate" the area which, had in recent years been undergoing a depression due to the re location of the many heavy engineering and chemical industries which had been the mainstay of the region's economy. The focal point of the regeneration was East Manchester which had been the worst affected. The Cambridge Policy Consultants estimate that the Games will help to regenerate approximately 60ha of land and create 72,000m of employment floor space in East Manchester (Cambridge Policy Consultants, 2002). The image of the region seems to have been greatly improved by the games, with 18 million people visiting the region in 2002 putting £6 billion into the North West's economy, and with over 300,000 expected each year (Regeneration/ Legacy. www.gameslegacy.com). The wish to host an event of this kind does not derive from a sense of philanthropy or love of sport, but is now largely seen as a business opportunity. The games act like a magnet, attracting attention, which in turn transforms into the more tangible investment and increased tourism.

Qatar, host of the 2006 Asian Games, has spent an

estimated $17 billion on the development of new sports, tourism and cultural facilities. The games were seen as an opportunity to launch Qatar as a major tourist and financial hub. Thus what one sees is that these hallmark events tend to serve as a "spotlight", focusing the world's attention on the host city. This often results in improved infrastructure for the cities' citizens, as well as increased interest in the city as an investment destination.

This is one of the themes than one sees recurring in a number of bids for the games. Cape Town in its failed 2004 Olympics bid highlighted the urban regeneration, and socio-economic impact that the event would have. The Cape Town 2004 Olympic bid was designed to be developmental, with every aspect of the plan attempting to contribute to the "upliftment" of those previously disadvantaged under apartheid.

The costs of these mega-events almost always run in to billions of dollars. Japan spent over $4 billion, and South Korea $2 billion, on new stadiums and infrastructure for the 2002 World Cup. China has spent a reported $20 billion on infrastructure improvements ahead for 2008 Olympics. Athens spent over $1 billion only on security expenses during the 2004 Olympics (Baade, R and Matheson, V, 2003).

Substantial economic impact provides backers of such events with a justification for public subsidies for mega-event infrastructure. They argue that the expenditure must be viewed as an investment that will in turn give returns. However this is a case where vested interests are at stake. Many independent researchers have found that ex ante predictions made by the event organizers of economic impact, far exceed the ex post estimates. The obvious question that results from this, is the cost justified, is yet to be answered conclusively either way.

This brings us to another interesting development, the arrival of developing nations on the sportshosting scene. Developing nations have only hosted two summer Olympics, one Winter Olympics, one Commonwealth Games and six football World Cups. This of course, due to the changing world order and rising prominence, is set to change. Beijing has host the 2008 Summer Olympics, India, the 2010 Commonwealth Games, South Africa the 2010 Football World Cup and South Asia the 2011 Cricket World Cup. However research seems to point out that though the benefits of hosting these events are dubious at best, the factors seem to work expressly against developing nations. The experience that a developing nation faces is vastly different from that of a developed nation. This is especially pertinent in the Indian context as we prepare to host the 2010 Commonwealth Games, and make a push to host the 2014 Asian Games, and the 2016 Olympic Games.

As Matheson and Baade (2003) point out, there are very good reasons for why developing nations are more adversely impacted by such events. They can be listed as:

1. High infrastructure development costs.
2. Under-utilization of facilities post-event
3. High opportunity cost of capital
4. Unable to attract large numbers of spectators.

The first factor that works against developing nations is the lack of existing infrastructure. In order to host the 1994 World Cup, the United States spent less than $30 million on sports infrastructure improvements, compared to over $2 billion spent by South Korea for the 2002 World

Cup. For the 1982 Asian Games in New Delhi, only one pre- existing stadium was used, while all the rest were new.

The development of professional sporting leagues with dedicated followings in developed nations means that post event; the facilities can be utilized efficiently. The expenditure on these facilities is exceedingly large, and for them to be good public investments, efficient post event usage is crucial. In developing nations these facilities are beneficial as they provide world-class facilities for athletes in that country. However it is also seen that in such nations, facilities tend to be grossly underutilized.

Bureaucracy and the lack of a developed sports economy means that these "world-class" are not only inefficiently used post- event but also tend to fall into disrepair. One need not look far for an example, all over one sees sports infrastructure developed for the 1982 Asian Games lying derelict and unused. After the 2002 football World Cup, teams from the Japanese football league, J-League, moved into the new stadiums while South Korea on the other hand had few plans for the new stadia. Nigeria' government recently spent $330 million on a new national soccer stadium, more than the annual national government expenditures on health or education. In developing nations the opportunity cost of developing sports infrastructure is very high, as the money can be used for more pressing needs. Even though Japan spent an estimated $6 billion in the run up to the World Cup, there was little criticism as the economy was suffering a recession and the government had committed itself to high public expenditure, making the opportunity cost of capital practically zero.

Developed nations may also be able to attract a larger number of spectators compared to developing nations where residents may be unwilling to pay the high ticket costs or where a sporting culture is not highly developed. In the 2002 World Cup, Japanese stadiums were filled to 89.1% capacity for its 32 games while Korean stadiums achieved only a 78.8% capacity, this even though the South Korean team did surprisingly well, boosting sales.

All the factors do not work against developing nations. Low wages, meaning lower operational costs, general infrastructure improvements and a low opportunity cost of labour all factors that work in their favour. However the evidence seems to suggest that the economic effects of such events, especially in the case of developing nations, is not always as positive as the event organizers would have us believe.

This is something we need to keep in mind as India attempts to make a mark in the world-sporting map by hosting the 2010 Commonwealth Games, and makes a push for the 2014 Asian Games and the 2016 Olympics. We should well heed the advice given by the same authors. Cities and countries would be well advised to more thoroughly evaluate booster promises of a financial windfall from hosting a sports me ga-event such as the World Cup and Olympics before committing substantial public resources to such an event. Indeed, hosting these premier events may be more of a burden than an honor.

1982 saw the return of the Asian Games to its original home, New Delhi. The first edition of the Asian Games had been held in 1951 with eleven participating nations and six competitive sports. By 1982, the games had grown manifold with 33 nations and nearly 4600 athletes and officials participating in 21 sports and 147 events, the largest ever Asian Games.2The games had grown to be the second largest sporting event in the world, second only to the Summer Olympics.

The 1982 Games was the first time after independence that the country was playing host to an international event of this magnitude. The world's attention was about to be focused on the city and it was not going to disappoint. The games were an announcement to the world that India had arrived. The games seem to have a very deep felt impact on the country as a whole, interestingly in many arenas far removed from sport.

It is pertinent to note that 1982 Asiad almost didn't take place at all. Though India had won the bid to host the games in 1976, by 1980 no work had even started and the Games surely looked doomed. There had been a change of government in-between and a lot of political turmoil had plagued the country in those years. In 1980, Indira Gandhi was back in power, and she along with her son Rajiv Gandhi, made it her personal mission to pull off a successful games. The city was to be prepared to host the largest event it had ever experienced, along with build numerous stadiums, flyovers, hotels and the Games Village in a span of 20 months.

That the Asian Games Special Organising Committee (SOC) was able to pull it off is commendable, though there were numerous shortcomings as well. Buildings like the player's building and the roof of the Talkatora swimming pool weren't completed on time, development was haphazard and short sighted, and there was little importance given to planning norms and regulations. There is little information pertaining to the Asian Games available in the public domain, and the little that does remain is scattered among the tens of government organisations that dealt with the event. It is therefore also nearly impossible to get an accurate picture of the total expenditure on the games, though estimates seem to place it at between 7-10,000 million rupees, a sum a nation as poor as India could hardly afford. At the same time, revenues were almost negligible. The SOC made about 60 million rupees through ticket sales, donations and franchising revenue, a sum not even enough to cover the operational costs of 150 million.3 Foreign tourists, who were supposed to enter the city in the thousands, never materialised. Only an estimated 200 arrived, leaving hotels and restaurants empty.

Economics and planning were often put aside as all trumpeted the notion of "international prestige". The Games had become an emotive issue, and anyone raising questions about it was unpatriotic and a traitor. One notices this in such events worldwide, where the backers of such events make it a nationalistic issue whereby it is unpatriotic to ask any questions, even when what is at stake is billions of dollars.

No queremos goles, queremos frijoles (we do not want goals, we want beans) was painted on a Mexico stadium during the Football World Cup in 1986 (Andreff, 2008). That statement in some way reflects the scenario in India in 1982 as well. The nation was still a heavily protected and closed economy, reeling under babudom and unable to shake off the "hindu" rate of growth.

"Hypocrisy and cynicism are even more evident than usual in New Delhi. The crores being spent on Asiad, The Asian Games of 1982, stand out in sharp relief against the real requirements of the people... The twisted values involved in advertising the luxuries and choice of expensive dishes available in five star hotels when millions are in search of food... descriptions of spacious air-conditioned suites each fitted with colour television sets. and other luxuries, appear side by side in the newspapers with grim reports of near famine conditions in large parts of the country". (*Indian Express,* October 30, 1982).

The famine conditions were not very far from the sight of the capital city itself. The construction spree that took place required workers, lakhs of them, with over 1.5 lakh workers working on sites directly related to the games, with many more on other construction projects. These workers were often paid lower than minimum wages, and forced to live in temporary jhuggies that a large majority never moved out of. Homeless people also reported that harassment increased, as there was a need to "clean up" the streets for the Asian Games, when the Bombay Prevention of Begging Act was used liberally to remove many hundreds of people from the streets of Delhi.

Any old timer in the city will tell you that it was in 1982 that Delhi finally began to "develop". The build up to the games saw an unprecedented construction spree in the city with stadiums, the games village, hotels, flyovers and roads, even Pragati Maidan being built, all with 1982 as the deadline. The skyline of the city literally changed overnight. Very few records remain on the public domain of the actual details of the construction that took place during that period, and few, if no, studies seem to have been conducted on the Games' impact.

The construction at the time can be broadly categorised into four groups:

1. Stadiums- The Jawaharlal Nehru Stadium was the centrepiece of the games, being the venue for the opening and closing ceremonies and athletics. The other major stadiums built at the time were the Talkatora Stadium, the Indira Gandhi Indoor

stadium and the Yamuna Velodrome. One notices that with the exception of the National Stadium, which was an earlier construction, most of the venues for the 1982 Games were new constructions.

2. Asiad Village- The Games village, where all the participating athletes and officials were to stay was a large project developed in the Siri Fort area.
3. Hotels- A number of hotels came up at the time like the Kanishka, the Mughal Sheraton and The Taj Palace.

The unprecedented nature of the construction involved for the games meant that the Master Plan, a broad outline for the planned development of the city, was largely sidelined in the name of "national prestige" (Baviskar, 2005). Normal planning procedures for land use changes and development were largely sidelined and nationalistic fervour meant they often won in the face of opposition from critics. The other aspect which meant that planning was often put on the back seat was the fact that the entire infrastructure for the games were largely built in the last 2 years leading up to the games, and not the 4-6 years that a country normally takes to prepare itself for an event of this size (Sisodia, 2005). Internal unrest and infighting had meant that the development of infrastructure had been left right to the last minute.

Though thousands of crores were spent at the time to develop world-class stadiums, the construction undertaken for the games was largely of a shoddy and poor quality, reflecting the haste in which they were built. The Player's building was never completed, nor was the roof of the Talkatora swimming pool. The retracting roof of the Indira Gandhi indoor stadium hailed as a technological feat never worked effectively and even after numerous repairs, the roof still leaks. An international Badminton competition in the 1990's was disrupted due to water leaking in. The main stadium, built on the banks of the Yamuna is actually tilting on one side. The Delhi High Court also sealed the main portion of the stadium, as it does not fulfil fire safety norms (Venugopal, 2005).

The adjoining Yamuna Velodrome is in a pathetic state with the velodrome full of cracks and bumps, and more often visited by snakes and rats than humans. The Nehru Stadium too is crumbling and bad maintenance means that even though new tracks were laid recently, they are already in disrepair. Utilisation of those stadiums has also not been very high. Bad maintenance has meant that they cannot be used for high profile international events and even domestic events are not held very often.

The stadiums do serve as training grounds for the Sports Authority of India (SAI) but the fact remains that these stadiums have not been used to capacity since 1982. The stadiums are used more often for Bollywood events or political rallies than sporting events. Recently the only high profile international event that the famed J.N. Stadium has been used for is the Half Marathon where it was the starting and end point! There are therefore some hard questions that must be answered about the "legacy" that such events create. Numerous stadiums were built in 1982 but not a single one has been maintained appropriately and therefore none of them has been used effectively. It is quite apparent that these stadiums are simply given a facelift in the run up to an event but otherwise left in a state of disrepair. This also means that the domestic athletes training there do not have up to the mark facilities.

The core of the Asian games was the village that was

developed by the DDA, in the Siri Fort area. The design of the Games village, by noted architect, Raj Rewal, was considered a great success and revolutionary in its "cluster" approach to housing. The complex was taken over as government housing post-event, soon becoming a much-coveted address among government and PSU officials. The development of this site probably had the largest urban impact on the city due to its correlation with the development of south Delhi. South Delhi was a region that had already begun being developed, but it was only after the 1982 games that saw this region increase in importance. Three of the four flyovers developed at the time, the Moolchand, Sewa Nagar and Oberoi flyovers were in south Delhi. The city, which had been growing rapidly, was running out of space and this region seemed perfect for development. The area where the village was developed, Siri Fort, was originally a Master Plan green but at this time was reallocated for the use of the village. The reason that the games had such a deep impact on the development in south Delhi was because they provided the region with the necessary infrastructure to develop.

It provided the region with broad roads and flyovers for swift movement of traffic and other infrastructure as well such as water, electricity and other civic amenities. The other large residential complex built at the time was the Player's Building, which was envisaged a VIP complex meant for senior officials and visitors during the games. The Players' Building wasn't finished on time and remained uninhabited for 15 years, till it was reborn as the Delhi Secretariat.

The hotels built at the time were largely government owned and operated. The state of government hotels need not be enumerated here but it is widely accepted that they were mostly money losing ventures. These hotels hardly ever rose above occupancy rates of 40%, mostly propped up by government and PSU conferences filling up rooms. The government hotels are mostly in a sorry state, though privatisation, like the new Shangri-La has saved some from complete ruin.

No doubt, broader roads and flyovers were welcome additions to the cities crumbling infrastructure at the time, easing congestion and quickening transit times. They were however biased in their location as they were all built with the purpose of serving the '82 games, meaning that they were not located in the most congested places which needed them most but on routes which the athletes would take between stadiums and the games village. The ring roads too were further broadened at the time, roads which are now the lifeline of the city. The four flyovers built at the time also led to tens more being built during the '80s and '90s drastically easing congestion even in the face of ever increasing numbers on the road.

The ring road is today virtually stopless with almost all traffic lights on the route being eliminated through flyovers. The effect of an event of this magnitude on the environment can be quite detrimental, increasing pollution and causing imbalances by rampant, unchecked development. Unfortunately little research seems to have been undertaken at the time. One can point out however that certain areas, which were originally planned to be green open areas for the city, were developed at the time. Also further portions of the Ridge area, a no build zone, were encroached upon. The duration of the games also saw a rise in the lead concentration in the air, probably due to the rise in automobiles on the roads at the time (Boralkar, Mukharjee, and Singh, 1986).

One implication of an event like this taking place in the city, especially pertinent in the Indian context is the fact that it sets a deadline for projects. In the words of a senior DDA official, all the projects like roads, flyovers and hotels would have taken place even without the games, it's just that they would have taken 10 years instead of the 2 that they did. This comment is very true in the Indian context where construction often takes years and years with no end in sight. The games were able to fix a date before which the project must be completed which ensured that construction did not slacken. This is even more apparent when seen in the context of the introduction of colour television. In the build up to the games there was a decision taken to broadcast the games in colour. This gave DD the impetus to almost overnight upgrade their existing technology to support this, an up gradation that might have otherwise taken years.

The Asian Games was in some senses a landmark event in the country with far reaching implications. The games had an impact on areas as diverse as the Khalistan movement to the judicial process in the country to television broadcasting. Some of the interesting impacts are enumerated below. By 1982, the Khalistan movement was already well under way. In an attempt to highlight their condition, protest marches were scheduled in Delhi during the games. In an attempt to counter this, the government took a tough stand, rounding up Sikhs all over the country and in the capital. No Sikhs were allowed to proceed towards Delhi and all means of transport were monitored. Bhajan Lal, the Chief Minister of Haryana took an exceptionally strong stand, not allowing the movement of Sikhs in the state. Many Sikhs, even those with reason to travel to Delhi were roughed up, further embittering them. S. Khushwant Singh, speaking in the Parliament on the

President's Address, warned that the country would have to pay a heavy price for the treatment meted out to Sikhs during the Asiad. He warned the government, "Was it ever realised that in so doing the government embittered thousands of Sikhs and played into the hands of Akali extremists by confirming their charge of governmental discrimination against the Sikhs? If, God forbid, the Khalistan movement catches on, it will owe much to the foolish short-sightedness of Bhajan Lal". Thus in some ways, the Asiad can be seen as a major factor in the rise of anti-government sentiment among the Sikhs.

Similarly, the construction frenzy that preceded the Asian Games, lakhs of workers entered the city, increasing the population of the city from 55 lakh to 65 lakh (approx., Source-Dunnu Roy) in a span of a few years. These workers were forced to stay in cheap temporary housing, which most of them never moved out of, and receive below minimum wage pay. In a landmark case, the Asiad worker's case (Peoples' Union for Democratic Rights Vs. Union of India, AIR 1982 SC 1473), filed by the People's Union for Democratic Rights (PUDR), the Supreme Court allowed what has now become known as Public Interest Litigation (PIL).

Thus one of the first PIL's, a tool often used by concerned citizens now, was filed on behalf of the Asiad workers. This case was seminal in the context of the minimum wages act as it held a person receiving less than minimum wage, a bonded labourer. The court ruled, "Where a person provides labour or service to another for remuneration which is less than minimum wage, the labour or service provided by him clearly falls within the scope and ambit of the word 'forced labour"..." All labour rewarded with less than the minimum wage, then, constitutes forced labour and violates the Constitution of India (Sreenath, Sreenath, and Student Group, 2005).

The Supreme Court held that a person who provides service to another for less than the minimum wage renders forced service, i.e. "begar" within the meaning of Article 23 of the constitution. This ruling was very important in the workers fight against exploitation, and ensured that non-payment of minimum wages would be considered a serious offence and viewed as a violation of the Constitution of India.

One of the most visible effects of the Asian Games was the advent of colour television. To promote the games, the government directed DD to air the games in colour, and also allowed the import of colour TVs, a big policy change in those protectionist days. The Asian Games also led to the setting up of the Department of Sport, now the Ministry of Youth Affairs and Sports, and the National Informatics Centre (NIC) the body responsible for providing network backbone and e-Governance support to Central Government, State Governments, UT Administrations, Districts and other Government bodies (Sisodia, 2005).

4

Commenwealth Games 2010: Glimpses of Infrastructure Development

The New Delhi is on its way to become a global city by the year 2010. As the idea may seem improbable to any Delhiite, it is not. The signs of a bright future are already visible with the infrastructural development on the rise. As 2010 Commonwealth Games are around the corner, the development on the various fronts have been expedited in the past few years. Once the plans are implemented, the city will be finally amongst the great metropolises of the world.

Infrastructure Development

The city boasts of modern elements of infrastructure like pollution checks, mass rapid transit and state-of-the-art highways. To give a makeover to the city for Commonwealth Games, the Indian Government is shelling out $17.5 billion on overall civic infrastructure. New streets and roads, overall city modernization, city beautification, development of public transport, new power plants, water supply services, Games Village, good connectivity, traffic management, security services and health services are some of the elements on which the works are underway.

The expansion of Delhi's Rapid Mass Transit System (Delhi Metro) is underway to cater to more passengers and boost public transportation. By the year 2010, Delhi Metro will be world's second largest network.

Indira Gandhi International (IGI) Airport is undergoing a major makeover. A new two tier terminal – Terminal 3 – will be operational by the 2010 Games. This will serve more than 35 million people a year. The bottom level of this terminal will be used for arrivals while the top level will be that of departures area. With high-end devices and sophistications, the facility will match global standards. A new runway will also be operational to handle more than 75 flights per hour. With a length of 4.4-km, this runway will be one of Asia's longest.

A 4-lane, 2.2 km long tunnel from Ring Road to Lodhi Road will link Games Village to the Jawaharlal Nehru Stadium. The tunnel will reduce traveling time for athletes by 6 minutes. High Capacity Bus System will be introduced by year 2010. Six corridors with a total length of 115 km have been identified for which around Rs 1000 crore has been earmarked. By the year 2009, 10,000 buses will be replaced with new vehicles which will have pneumatic doors and low floorboards to ensure easy boarding and de-boarding as well as an automatic vehicle tracking system connected to GPS for monitoring purposes.

Integrated Rail Bus Transit System project is also proposed which will connect the capital with its suburbs.

In view of large number of trains passing daily by Delhi region, new road under-bridges and over-bridges are under construction along the railway lines. New cloverleafs, flyovers and bridges are under construction for providing connectivity to sports venues, Games Village, hotels and hospitals.

Road-widening projects are underway. Efforts are also underway to make both the inner and outer Ring Roads signal free. A 225-km-long "Super Ring Road" around the periphery of the city is proposed.

To meet the power requirements and to provide additional power during the games, a mammoth power-production project is in the pipeline. This will increase production of electricity to 7000 MW from the current 4500 MW. Two new gas-based power plants are being constructed in Bawana and Pragati to achieve this end. It is expected that New Delhi will have surplus power. Load-shedding would be a term youngsters will need to look up in the dictionary.

Water and solid waste management are two areas for which New Delhi needs to work its socks off. Efforts are underway to improve on these fronts as well. Rainwater harvesting is another priority front to prepare for the water problem before it boils up into crisis.

Keeping an eye on 2010 Commonwealth Games, it is needless to say that New Delhi will be a better place with more hotels and restaurants, golf courses, swimming pools, leisure parks, health clubs, theaters, entertainment centers, global cuisine, multiplexes and shopping arcades which will definitely storm its cultural landscape. New Delhi is all set for the mega event. The signs are all there for Delhi to become a global megapolis.

2010 CWG GETS ADDITIONAL FUNDING

Government on Friday (18-Mar. 2010) decided to pump in another Rs 687.06 crore for the Commonwealth Games to install high-end equipment and fittings necessary for the sporting extravaganza.

The Union Cabinet presided by Prime Minister Manmohan Singh cleared the proposal from the Sports Ministry for "overlays" to be given to Organising Committee of Commonwealth Games which will be held here in October.

Overlays are defined as temporary fittings, fixtures and equipment which will be required only for the duration of the Games. They are required to make the competition, training and non-competition venues operationally ready for the Games.

"The installation of these high-end items of overlays will set high standards for technological excellence and capacity enhancement not only in the sphere of sports but also for the organisation and management of mega international and national events," I and B Minister Ambika Soni told reporters.

The overlays are expected to be in place and operational about a month prior to the Games, that is by the end of August and these will be removed from the venues immediately after the Games, she said.

This amount will be in addition to the Rs 2,296.43 crore allocation made for the Games in the Union Budget for next fiscal. Of this, Rs 2,069.52 crore has been allocated to Sports Ministry for the while Urban Development ministry has been given Rs 176.90 crore and Delhi government Rs 50 crore.

The Games will be held in the capital from October three to 14 in 17 sporting disciplines. There will be 23 competition venues, 26 training venues, Games Village,

International Broadcasting Centre and Main Press Centre among other facilities.

Around one lakh people are expected to visit the capital during the event. Soni said the competition and non-competition venues are in an advanced stage of construction by concerned agencies such as Delhi Government, Sports Authority of India and Delhi Development Authority.

The Timing, Scoring Result (TSR) system including the On Venue Result (OVR) system and Games Time Sports equipment are being separately procured by the Organising Committee, she said.

The security and surveillance related equipment at the venues is being installed by Electronic Corporation of India Ltd, she added.

DOORDARSHAN GETS GO-AHEAD FOR 2010 COMMONWEALTH GAMES HDTV TELECAST

Millions of Delhi residents, many already living below the poverty line, are to bear the brunt of a massive hole in the Commonwealth Games budget after the city unveiled huge tax hikes on consumer products from cooking gas to tea.

The city's 2010-2011 budget is likely to spark increasing resentment against the Commonwealth Games from residents already suffering from rising food prices caused by India's soaring inflation rates.

Announcing the unpopular budget measures, Delhi chief minister Sheila Dikshit sought to soothe anger over the price hikes, saying; "We need money for the Commonwealth Games".

> "I would appeal to the residents (of Delhi) to understand our position."

The Delhi government maintains it has been left with no choice but to saddle its residents with additional taxes because of a massive shortfall in expected central government funding for the October 4-13 event.

The city, which has undertaken a series of massive infrastructure development projects ahead of the Games, asked the Central Congress-led government for 2000 crore rupees ($480 million) last year but received only 50 crore ($120m). The new state tax rises will make up for more than half of the shortfall, raising an anticipated 1130 crore rupees.

The tax hikes will cover houschold goods as prosaic as plastic and tin containers, cutlery, cooking oil and gas and school bags, as well as luxury goods such as watches and dress pens.

But the impost likely to cause the most pain is the 7.5 per cent increase in the tax on diesel (from 12.5 per cent to 20 per cent) which analysts forecast yesterday would force up the price of all foods transported across the country.

Opposition parties yesterday condemned the budget as "looting in the name of the Commonwealth Games".

> "They are spending crores (tens of millions of rupees) on flower pots," Opposition Leader Vijay Kumar Malhotra said.
>
> "The whole city is being dug up . . . the people of Delhi are being crushed in the name of the Games."

The sporting event is transforming the city in ways not universally popular among the estimated 16 million residents.

While it is hoped a city-wide subway system now under

construction will transform Delhi's choked and chaotic roads, thousands of the city's poorest have also been displaced as slums have been demolished to make way for the Games village.

Doordarshan gets go-ahead for 2010 Commonwealth Games HDTV telecast On July 30, 2009, the Union Cabinet given the go-ahead to allow Doordarshan to telecast the 2010 Commonwealth Games in high definition Television (HDTV) format. The cabinet has approved a Rs 1.65 billion budget in the 11th plan allocation of Prasar Bharati, for the upgrade to HDTV.

With the funding, Doordarshan will be able to upgrade its infrastructure in Delhi, Mumbai, Kolkata, and Chennai to telecast the Commonwealth Games in HDTV format.

> *indiatelevision.com* has reported that the requisite equipment will have to be imported at a cost of around Rs 1.6 billion. The remaining Rs 50 million has been earmarked for recurring expenditure for project implementation and spectrum charges.

Reports say that the Information and Broadcasting (I&B) ministry has shortlisted five broadcasters, namely, Tokyo Broadcasting, Canadian Broadcasting Corporation, USA's International Sports Broadcasting and International Games Broadcast Services.

As of now Prasar Bharati's transmitters are largely on analog mode. The HDTV format will enable Prasar Bharati to provide superior picture and sound quality to viewers. Though, viewers will need HDTV-enabled TVs or a set-top box to view the programming in HDTV.

Meanwhile, in other news about the 2010 Commonwealth Games, the Supreme Court of India overturned a Delhi High Court ruling that required the setting up of a committee to monitor the construction at the Commonwealth Games Village (CGV) in Delhi.

As per the Supreme Court judgment, the Delhi Development Authority (DDA) can now continue to build the CGV.

"Delhi Development Authority (DDA) and other authorities are free to proceed with the work at the CWG village site," the Supreme Court said.

The High Court ruling had come after a petition was made that the construction of the CGV would have an adverse effect on the ecology of the Yamuna river bed that would lead to the changing of the river's course causing flooding.

The High Court then gave the directive that a committe should be set up to ascertain whether the CGV site complex was, in fact, being built on the Yamuna riverbed or flood plain.

The DDA appealed to the Supreme Court against the ruling saying that the project had received environmental clearances including that from National Environmental Engineering Research Institute (NEERI).

The DDA also pointed out that that the Akshardham Temple was built 1.7 km away from the Yamuna river bed and that the CGV site was situated 1.2 kms away from the river bed.

It also said that the stalling of the project just some time away from the 2010 Commonwealth games would jeopardize its sovereign guarantee for holding the 2010 Commonwealth Games in Delhi. The government has already pumped in Rs 2,000 into the project, and is already behind schedule.

The Supreme Court accepted this and said the construction site of the CGV site was adjacent to that of the Akshardham Temple complex, and therefore the same considerations should be applied to the building of the CGV.

The Supreme Court bench comprising Chief Justice K.G. Balakrishnan and Justices P. Sathasivam and B.S. Chauhan upheld the appeal and said the observation and conclusion of the High Court was unsustainable.

"The decision of the expert and autonomous body, NEERI, supported by materials placed by other bodies such as Central Water Power Research Station and the ministry of environment and forest (MoEF), the same cannot be lightly interfered with by the court without adequate contra material," Justice Sathasivam, the author of the judgment, said.

> The bench also held that the High Court had not taken into consideration of experts and scientific organisations that have categorically maintained that the CGV site is not located on a riverbed or a flood plain.

The Supreme Court also said that the High Court should not have entertained the PIL since it was file in 2007, eight years after the land was alloted in 1999.

The apex court also set aside the committee that was put together by the High Court to examine the construction of the CGV from an ecological vantage point.

Meanwhile, a special commissioner of police was appointed by the government, for the 2010 Commonwealth

Games, on July 28, 2009. The new commissioner of police, Ajay Chadha, was transferred from Arunachal Pradesh where he was Director General of Police.

HOTEL ROOMS FOR TOURISTS IN HARYANA

The Tourism Department of Haryana is readying to provide the best services possible to the foreigners visiting India for the Commonwealth Games 2010, to be held in New Delhi, according to Kumari Selja, Union Minister for Tourism, Housing and Urban Poverty Alleviation.

She told reporters in Ambala in Haryana that as many as 6,000 rooms are being constructed "on a war-footing" by the various hotel-owners in Haryana. All these rooms will be completed within the stipulated time, she added.

The Minister said that vehicle drivers will be given "behavioural training" on how to "behave decently" with the foreign tourists and others coming to New Delhi for the Commonwealth Games.

The road tax of different states will be collected at one point in order to make it easy for the tourists who would be visiting other states. Later, the road tax so collected will be distributed among the states concerned, Kumari Selja said.

A special campaign is at present under way to promote tourism in the Ambala parliamentary constituency. Holistic schemes, the Minister said, will be drawn up after examining the tourism potential in Ambala, Yamunnagar, and Panchkula.

The Common Wealth Games 2010, according to Kumari Selja, is expected to boost India's tourism sector considerably. This will be the biggest sports event to be held in India so far. The Haryana government has already announced that, for the Common Wealth Games 2010, a "bed-and-breakfast scheme" will be implemented in Gurgaon. According to this scheme, house-owners can rent out their premises to tourists.

Rajender Kataria, Deputy Commissioner of Gurgaon, said that since it takes a long time to construct a hotel, the Central Government has approved about 25 houses in Gurgaon which could be converted into guesthouses. The registration and other legal process related to these guesthouses have been simplified, and adequate security will be provided to the buildings where the tourists stay.

Because the hotel industry is suffering from a financial crunch and the real estate sector from the downturn, the bed-and-breakfast scheme appears to be the only viable alternative, according to Rajender Kataria. Efforts are being made to make available other services such as conference rooms and restaurants.

Under the bed-and-breakfast scheme, house-owners are allowed to rent out a maximum of 5 rooms, along with complimentary services such as power backup, airconditioning, Wi-Fi, as well as 24X7 security.

The Haryana government will market the bed-and-breakfast facility online.

5

Gates of Delhi

Delhi is known for its gates. The Gates of Delhi were built in Delhi, India, under different dynastic rulers in the period that could be dated from eighth century to twentieth century. These are: i) the gates of the ancient city of Lal Kot or Qila Rai Pithora, also called the first city of Delhi (period 731-1311) in Mehrauli – Qutb Complex; ii) the gates in the second city of Siri Fort (1304); iii) the gates in the third city Tughlaqabad (1321–23), iv) the gates in the fourth city of Jahanpanah's of (mid 14th century); v) the gates in the fifth city of Feruzabad (1354); vi) the sixth city of Dilli Sher Shahi (Shergarh) 's gates (1534); near Purana Qila; vii) the gates built in the seventh city Shahjahanabad of (mid 17th century); and viii) the gates in the eighth modern city New Delhi of British Raj (1931s) in Lutyens' Delhi of the British rule.

In 1611, the European merchant William Finch had described Delhi as the city of seven castles (forts) and fifty two gates. More gates were built after that period also during the Mughal rule and during the British rule. But, as on date, only 13 gates exist in good shape, while all others are in ruins or have been demolished. Like all gates denote, the direction of the destination station is the starting name of the gate.

Gates in the First City

In the first city of Delhi, 13 gates were built in the 11th century citadel of Lal Kot, with the extended Qila Rai Pithora, which was ruled by the Slave Dynasty from 1192 with the establishment of the Qutb complex. These were located in the rubble built ramparts of Lal Kot (5–6 m (16–20 ft)) thickness) of which only a few remain, either in ruins or under renovation. These are the Chaumukha, Sohan, Ranjit, Fateh, Hauz Rani, Barka, Badaun and Budayuni gates. Of these, the Chaumukha, Ranjit, Sohan and Fateh darwazas have been listed by the INTACH as heritage monuments. The ruins of Hauz Rani and Barka are seen around the remains between giant gaps in the long stretches of the Lal Kot wall, surrounded by a wide moat on the outside. Archeological Survey of India (ASI) has proposed to conserve all the identified gates.

The Chaumukha Darwaza, is inferred as the gate way of Lal Kot since it aligns with Lal Kot walls. It is located near the Qutb Complex and has been categorized as Grade B in archaeological value. It has been conserved by the ASI. The gate's architectural style is also traced to the Tuglaq period in view of its massive thickness. It has a "horned" outwork with paved stones in an engraved grid pattern that indicates that it was designed for defense purposes. The purpose for which it was built has not been discerned. Hence, it has also been conjectured that it could have been built by Thomas Metcalfe as one of his follies, close to his original 'Dilkusha' mansion (now seen in ruins) to enhance the elegance of his retreat.

The Ranjit gate towards the north wall of Lal Kot is in ruins. It was once considered as a grand gate through which the Turks had entered the city. Hence, it was subsequently fortified to prevent any further foreign incursions. At present, only part of the gate is seen and is yet to be listed as a heritage monument.

The Fateh Gate close to Fateh Burj has convoluted features and is about(24 m (79 ft)) in diameter. The Sohan Gate guarded by a large bastion called the Sohan Burj was stated to be the location of a Sun temple.

Hauz Rani and Budayuni Gates, which were reportedly once prominent gates, are now traced in ruins. An interesting anecdote of history of the Budayuni gate, considered then as the principal gate of the city by Ibn Battuta (the chronicler of the period, mentions it as the main gate to the city), is that Allauddin Khilji had resolved to shun drinking of alcohol by emptying his wine caskets and breaking his rich Chinaware at this gate. The gate was also known for punishment meted out to the guilty. They were tortured and beheaded in public view at this gate. A strict watch was maintained at this gate to detect and prevent incursions by Mongolians.

Alauddin Khilji had planned, as part of his ambitious architectural achievements, to build four darwazas (gates) but he could build only one during his life time, namely the Alai Darwaza (1311). This gate is seen at the southern end of the Qutb complex of the enlarged Quwwat-ul-Islam mosque, built entirely on the principles of Islamic architecture. The gate made of rectangular bands of red sandstone and white marble has inscriptions of verses from Koran and Hadis in elaborate carvings on its windows. It is a square building- (17.2 m (56 ft)) square with dome with horse shoe pointed shaped arches on three sides and with a semicircular arch on the northern side. The underside of the arches have fringed lotus bud embellishments.

Historian Fanshawe writing euphorically on the beauty of the gate has extolled:

> The Alai Darwaza is not only the most beautiful structure at the Kutub, but is one of the most striking specimens of external polychromatic decoration not merely in India, but in the whole world, while the carving of interior may challenge comparison with any work of the kind. Both exterior and interior merit detailed and leisurely examination. The effect of the graceful pointed arches in the three external sides of the gate, and in the corner recesses is extremely pleasing, and the view from the exterior through the southern archway to the round-headed arch of the north side, and the court beyond, is very striking. The decoration of the north arch is curious and unique. The effect of exterior suffers, from a distant point of view, from the absence of a parapet above the walls; this was unfortunately removed by Captain Smith, as it was greatly ruined. The gate was finished five years before the emperor died, and is specially mentioned by the chronicler of his reign.

Gates in the Second City

The second medieval city of Siri Fort was built during the rule of Ala-ud-Din Khalji of the Delhi Sultanate with the major objective of protecting the city from the onslaught of the Mongols. The city, when built with an oval plan, was best described as presenting an embodiment of richness with palaces and other structures and had seven gates for entry and exit. But, at present, only the Southeastern gate exists, also in ruins (pictured). The destruction of the fort and its gates are attributed more to the local rulers of subsequent dynasties who removed the stones, bricks and other artifacts of the fort for their own buildings and palaces.

Gates in the Third City

Tughlaqabad, the third city of medieval Delhi, built by Ghazi Malik well known as Ghiyath al-Din Tughluq who established the Tughlaq Dynasty in 1321 after ousting the Khiljis, was enclosed within a fort of massive proportions completed in a short span of four years. The fort has inclined walls with triple storied citadels, enormous towers, mosques and halls. The city when built is stated to have had 52 gates but only 13 remain today, mostly in ruins. Of the remaining gates, the main entry gate to the fort was built in typical Pathan style, which is described as made of red sand stone with sloping face and jambs which merge well with the towers of the fort. But the fort was abandoned soon after Ghiyasuddin's death for two reasons namely, water shortage and the fool hardy decision of his successor Sultan, the Muhammad bin Tughlaq who forcibly shifted his capital to the new city of Daulatabad in the Deccan and retuned back to found the fourth city of Jahanpanah.

Gates in the Fourth City

Muhammad bin Tughluq, first built Adilabad, then Nai-ka-Kot, towards the south of Tughlaqabad. These were two small fortresses. But he soon abandoned them. He built a new city by enclosing the areas lying between the cities of Siri, Tughlaqabad and Lal Kot. The city was named as Jahanpanah, asylum of the world, in 1334. The city had 13 gates. The ruins of gigantic ramparts of his two fortresses and some portions of the Jahanpanah walls have survived the ravages of time but are seen now only in total ruins. The watchtower Bijai Mandal still stands in ruins in the city of Jahanpanah. But no fort gates are traced

Gates in the Fifth City

Firuz Shah Tughlaq built a new capital city on the banks of the Yamuna River in 1351 and called it Firuzabad. The architecture of the fort was fairly simple and straightforward. The city had three palaces and a citadel known as Feroz Shah Kotla. The king's as well as his wife's quarters were situated along the riverfront. The structures within the enclosure walls of the fort were barracks, armories, servant's rooms, halls for audience, an imposing mosque as well as public and private baths and a stepped well or baoli. An Ashokan pillar brought from Topara, Ambala was mounted on top of a pyramidal three-tiered construction. No gates of this period exist.

Gates in the Sixth City

Three main gates on the north, south and west are part of the fortifications of the Purana Qila, the sixth city of Delhi, built by Sher Shah Suri (1538–45). Sher Shah Suri raised his citadel after demolishing Dinpanah, the city built by Humayun. The fortifications of the Qila extended to a boundary of (2 km (1.2 mi)) on an irregularly oblong plan. Bastions adorned the corners and the western wall. Of the existing three gates, the west gate forms the entrance to the Qila and is called the Bara Darwaza (big gate). All three gates are double–storied structures built with red sandstone and have chhatris. The enclosure wall inside has cells in two–bay depth. The northern gate, built in 1543–44, is called the Talaqi-Darwaza for reasons unknown. On this gate, in the front, carved marble leogryphs in combat with a man are seen above the oriel windows. Built in random rubble masonry with dressed stone facing, the gate has a tall arch enclosed by two smaller arched openings. Two bastions adorn the gate with high ceiling rooms. On the second floor of the gate, there are two openings. Exterior surface of the gate had coloured tiles and the inner rooms were covered with incised plaster work. The Purana Qila was stated to have been left unfinished by Suri, which was later completed by Humayun. The southern gate is called the Humayun Darwaza; the reasons attributed for the name are that either Humayun built it or the gate overlooked Humayun's tomb. An inscription in ink on the gate refers to Sher Shah with the date as 950 A.H. (1543–44).

Sher Shah Gate

Sher Shah gate located to the south of Khairu'l-Manazil-Masjid is said to be an entrance to the large city of Delhi that Sher Shah built in front of his fortress of Purana Qila. The gate, mostly built with red sandstone but with use of local grey quartzite in its upper storey, is thus called the Lal Darwaza (red gate). Arcades were built from this gate into the city, which were provided with series of dwellings with frontage of a verandah, which may have been used for commercial establishments. Kabuli or Khuni–Darwaza (explained in the following section) is another gate on the fringes of Sher Shah's city. ASI has undertaken extensive conservation works of the gate and its surroundings at a cost of Rs 75 lakhs.

Gates in the Seventh City

It is pertinent to note that Shahjahanabad, the seventh city of Delhi, was built by Shah Jahan in 1649 like a fortress encircled by strong and high red–brick walls with 14 entry gates to the city, in addition to 16 wicket gates called windows (khirkis in Urdu language). A number of bastions built of stone were added by the British, in addition to repairing the earlier fort, to make the fort more secure. The gates were designed and built for the people to have access and the royal procession to enter or exit, when going out in diverse directions. Out of the 14 gates, five gates have survived, namely, the Kashmiri Gate on the north, the Ajmeri Gate on the south-west, the Delhi Gate on the south-east, Turkman Gate on the south and the Nigambodh Gate on the north-east, all of which express vividly the splendor of the city. All the gates are located within a radius of (5–6 km (3.1–3.7 mi)) in the present day Old Delhi. The Lahori gate on the Northeast, in the old city, was demolished (some remnant walls are seen at the crossing as may be seen in picture) and the area converted into the present day Lahori Bazar.

The gates have a square plan with high arched openings, except for low height of the Nigambodh gate, and two openings — one for entry and another for exit — of the Kashmiri gate. The names of all the gates, which existed during Shahajahan's time are the Dilli Darwaza (also known as Delhi Gate), Kabuli Darwaza, Raj Ghat Darwaza, Khizri Darwaza, Nigambodh Darwaza, Kela ke Ghat ka Darwaza, Lal Darwaza, Kashmiri Darwaza, Badar Darwaza, Patthar Khati Darwaza, Lahori Darwaza, Ajmeri Darwaza and Turkuman Darwaza. The names of the wicket gates or windows (now none exist) through which people entered and exited from the old fort city were: 1) Zeenatul Masajid Khirkee; 2) Nawab Ahmad Bakhsh ki Khirkee; 3) Nawab Ghaziuddin ki Khirkee; 4) Musamman Burj ki Khirkee; 5) Muslim Garh ki Khirkee; 6) Naseer Ganj ki Khirkee; 7) Nai Khirkee; 8) Shah Ganj Khirkee; 9) Ajmeri Darwaza ki Khirkee; 10) Sayyad Bhole ki Khirkee; 11) Buland Bagh ki Khirkee; 12) Farash Khana ki Khirkee; 13) Ameer Khan ki Khirkee; 14) Khalil Khan ki Khirkee; 15) Bahadur Ali Khan ki Khirkee; and 16) Nigambodh ki Khirkee. However, the Red Fort also has two gates namely, the Delhi gate and the Lahore gate, which are well maintained.

1. Kashmiri Gate

Kashmiri Gate is one of the original fourteen gates built into the wall to the north of the city. It was built by the British in 1835 by Major Robert Smith. Local people also call it as Truckman gate. It has a square plan. There are two openings of the gate – one for entry and another for exit (pictured). During 1835, the British enlarged and straightened it into a two way gate as defensive measure against enemy attacks. In the present city setting, the gate is close to the Inter State Bus Terminals. It is now preserved as monument on the road to the Old Secretariat and the Delhi University. It was named as Kashmiri Gate since it was used by the Emperors to go through this gate on their visits to Kashmir and North India. It was also the historic venue of the intense fighting which took place in 1857, between the British army and the Indian freedom fighters. The fortifications of this gate were used to fire cannons at the British army encamped at Ludlow Castle. The freedom fighters gathered at a place close to the St. James Church to discuss war strategy. British troops fought fiercely at this gate and re– captured the city from mutinous Indian soldiers. During the war, the gate was badly damaged by the British to get control over Delhi. Subsequently, area surrounding the Kashmiri Gate became the commercial hub of Delhi, when the Civil Lines were developed by the British.

2. Delhi Gate

Delhi gate on the south east, so named because of its large size, was built by Emperor Shah Jahan in 1638 as part of the rubble–built high fort walls that encircled the Shahajahanabad. Shahajahanabad was the seventh city of Delhi on its southeast stretch. It was built in a polygonal shape and lead to other earlier cities of Delhi. It was built at the start of the Daryaganj. The road was also called the Thandi sadak (the cool street) as it was a tree lined avenue. The gate, square in plan, was built in sandstone and is an impressive and large structure. Near the gate entry, two stone carvings of elephants were erected. The Emperor used this gate to go to the Jama Masjid for prayer. The road from this gate passing through Daryaganj lead to the Kashmiri gate. A part of the fort wall to the east has been demolished to build the Old Delhi Railway Station while the wall to the west exists. It is now a heritage gate maintained by the ASI and roads on either side leads Daryaganj, goes to the Kashmiri gate with Jama masjid on the left and the Red Fort to its right.

3. Ajmeri Gate

Ajmeri Gate, built in 1644, to the south–west of Shahjahanabad with a square plan, has high arched openings. The Sepoy Mutiny or the first war of Indian Independence in 1857 was fought at this venue also. The road, through this gate, leads to the city of Ajmer in Rajasthan, and hence its name. A lovely park surrounds the gate. The madrasa of Nawab Ghaziuddin Bahadur and Anglo Arabic Senior Secondary School were located in the vicinity. At present, the old walls of the fort have been demolished and replaced by commercial buildings and residential complexes, but the gate on the west exists.

4. Turkman Gate

Turkman Gate, located to the southern edge of Shahajahanabad, is named after the Sufi Saint Hazrat Shah Turkman Bayabani. His tomb dated to 1240, before building of Shahjahanabad, is located to the east of the gate. It is approached from the Jawahar Lal Nehru Road, the old Circular Road, in the vicinity of the Ramlila Grounds.

It has a square plan with high arched openings. The tomb of Razia Sultan and Kali Masjid or Kalan Masjid are located in close proximity of the gate.

5. Red Fort Gates

Red Fort has two well maintained gates namely the Lahori gate and the Delhi gate The Lahori gate of the Old Delhi city (now only a bazaar square with small remnants at one end) links with the Lahore gate of the Red Fort enclosing the Lahori bazaar and the Chandni Chowk in a length of (1.6 km (0.99 mi)). The Lahore gate is the main gate to the Red fort and is named so since it is oriented towards Lahore in Pakistan. Delhi gate was the main entrance linking Red fort with the city but entry is now restricted since it provided access to a large army camp inside the Fort (since vacated). It is used by the public. It is said that during Aurangzeb's reign the beauty of both the gates was spoiled by adding bastions: "The vista like a veil drawn across the face of a beautiful woman". In the 1980s, the area became a security zone due to its use for Indian Independence Day celebrations on 15th August for the flag hoisting and delivering an address to the Nation by the Prime Minister of India from the ramparts of the Red Fort. This necessitated blocking of the gate's tower windows as a security measure to prevent any kind of stealthy sniper attacks. At that time, a Lift was also added to the gate for use by the Prime Minister.

6. Nigambodh Gate

It was built on the north eastern side of the Shahajahanabad. It is located on the Ring Road near the Yamuna Bazaar. It derives its name Nigambodh Ghat from the burial ground here. The etymology of Nigambodh is derived from Sanskrit words 'Nigam' which means the

"Ved" and 'bodh' means "knowledge", meaning realization of knowledge. According to a folk legend, Lord Brahma (the creator) took a bath in the Yamuna River at this ghat to recover his lost memory and by this act Brahma not only got back his memory but also remembered the place he had kept his sacred books. In the past, the gate was closer to the ghat and nearer to the Salimgarh Fort.

7. *Khooni Darwaza*

Khooni Darwaza, literally translated means "Bloody Gate", a "morbid sounding name", though not within the walls of the Shahajahan's fort. Its historic significance is linked with the 1857 War of Indian Independence. Located on the Mathura road opposite to the Ferozshah Kotla near Maulana Azad Medical College, it is an impressive double–storied structure. Its construction is credited to Sher Shah Suri's reign (though the fort walls of the Suri period have not been seen to extend to this gate). It was built largely with grey stone but red stones were also used in the frames of its windows. According to the recorded history of the 1857 war (also called the Mutiny of 1857), the sons of Bahadur Shah, the last Mughal Emperor (who had taken shelter in Humayun's tomb) were arrested by the British officer named Captain William Hudson and while taking them to the Red Fort shot them dead and displayed their body on this gate for public viewing. He justified his action by claiming that a crowd which had assembled to see their arrested princes was restive and fearing an attack from the crowd he shot the two princes. Their dead bodies were also displayed at the Chandni Chowk. The gate is also the location where Dara Shikoh's severed head was displayed. In the battle of succession for the throne of Delhi, Aurangzeb murdered his brother Dara Shikoh and hung his severed head at this gate. During the riots in 1947, after the

Partition of India, many refugees were murdered here as they were trying to reach Purana Qila for safety.

8. Bahadur Shahi Gate

Salimgarh Fort, which is now part of Red fort complex, was constructed on an island of the Yamuna River in 1546. But a gate called the Bahadur Shahi Gate for entry into the Fort from the northern side was constructed only in 1854–55 AD by Bahadur Shah Zafar, the last Mogul ruler of India. The gate was built in brick masonry with moderate use of red sandstone. The fort was used during the Uprising in 1857 and also as prison, which housed Zebunnisa, daughter of Aurangzeb; the British imprisoned the freedom fighters of INA. The layout of the Red Fort was organized to retain and integrate this site with the Salimgarh Fort through the Bahadur Shah Gate.

Gates in the Eighth City

Delhi became the capital of British India after the seat of power was shifted from Calcutta in 1911. With this shift, the new city of New Delhi was established and the sixth city of Shahajahanabad to its north became the Old Delhi. Based on the designs of Edwin Lutyens, New Delhi was built over a period of 20 years. One of the important land marks built during this period was the India Gate. Built in 1921, it is officially known as All India War Memorial (an arch) to the Indian soldiers killed in the World War I, the Northwest frontier operations of the same time and the 1919 Afghan fiasco. The Gate has an impressive stone arch of (42 m (138 ft)) height; the names of over 90,000 soldiers are engraved on it.

The base of the gate is built in red Bharatpur stone and displays a shallow domed bowl. The past tradition was to fill this bowl with oil and light it as a lamp on anniversaries but is no more practiced, instead an eternal flame burns below the arch. The eternal flame was added in 1970s in the arch of the Gate to honour the Unknown Soldier. The location is flanked by two uniformed soldiers. The place takes a carnival atmosphere in the evenings when it is well lighted and visitors flock to the gate. Also seen behind the India Gate is an impressive Chhatri, which displayed the statue of King George V till 1968.

This statue has been shifted to the Coronation Park, Delhi, which was the site of the declaration of the new capital of Delhi. The Chhatri is now devoid of any statue since there is a protracted discussion on which National leader's statue should be installed there. There is an impressive set of a large central steel gates flanked by asymmetrically designed smaller gates that provides entry into the Rashtrapati Bhavan (President's palace). A commemorative column called the 'Jaipur Column' with a "distinctly peculiar crown: a glass star springing out of bronze lotus blossom", is located midway between the entry gates and the Rashtrapati Bhavan.

REFERENCES

Anon (1997). *Dictionary of Islamic architecture: Delhi, the capital of India*. Asian Educational Services. p. 55–56.

Arundhati Basu (2004-06-26). "Wisps of the past through Dilli's golden gates". *The Times of India*.

Fanshawe.H.C (1998). *Delhi, Past and Present*. Asian Educational Services. pp. 1 to 8.

Mahtab Jahan (2004). "Dilli's gates and windows". MG The Milli Gazette Indian Muslims leading new paper.

Patrick Horton; Richard Plunkett and Hugh Fnlay (2002). *Delhi*. Lonely Planet. pp. 92–94.

Peck (2005). *Delhi - A thousand years of Building*. New Delhi: Roli Books Pvt Ltd..

Sharama, Y.D. (2001). *Delhi and its Neighbourhood.* New Delhi: Archeological Survey of India. pp. 22, 83–84.

"Siri Fort". http://www.indiaprofile.com/tourist-attractions/delhi/siri-fort/. Retrieved 2009-05-07.

6

Shopping and Utility Services

Below is a list of various shopping areas and malls in and around the Delhi metropolitan area.

Main Markets/Shopping Districts

1. Chowk
2. Dilli Haat
3. Hauz Khas
4. Green Park
5. Connaught Place
6. Greater Kailash
7. Janpath
8. Jhandewalan
9. South Extension
10. Tilak Nagar
11. Vasant Kunj
12. Vasant Vihar.

Wholesale Markets

1. Azadpur Mandi
2. Okhla Mandi

3. Mehrauli
4. Sadar Bazaar
5. Chandni Chowk
6. Khari Baoli
7. Ghanta Ghar
8. Bhajanpura

Shopping Malls

Delhi

- Ansal Plaza, Hudco Place
- Metro Walk Mall, Rohini
- Cross River Mall, Shahdara
- North Square Mall, Pitampura
- Select Citywalk, Saket
- West Gate Mall
- TDI Mall Rajouri Garden, New Delhi
- City Square Rajouri Garden, New Delhi
- TDI Paragon Shivaji Place District Centre, Rajouri Garden, New Delhi
- The India Mall, New Friends Colony
- Emporio Mall, Vasant Kunj
- V3S East Centre Mall, Laxmi Nagar
- Vasant Square Mall, Vasant Kunj
- West Gate Mall, Shivaji Place

Ghaziabad

- Ansal Plaza, Vaishali
- East Delhi Mall, Kaushambi

- Pacific Mall, Kaushambi
- Shipra Mall, Indirapuram
- East End Mall, Kaushambi
- MMX Mall, Mohan Nagar
- Shopprix Mall, Kaushambi
- Silver City, G.T. Road
- Shopprix Mall, Vaishali Sector 5

Gurgaon

- DLF City Center Mall Gurgaon
- DLF Grand Mall Gurgaon
- DLF Mega Mall Gurgaon
- DLF Star Mall Gurgaon
- Galaxy Mall
- MGF Mega City Mall
- MGF Metropolitan Mall
- Sahara Mall
- Gold Souk
- MGF Plaza
- Ambience Mall
- Raheja Mall
- Marriage Mall
- Mall of India
- SRS Mall
- The Wedding Mall Gurgaon
- The ARDEE Mall
- Vishal Mega Mart

- Senior Mall
- Senior Auto Mall Gurgaon
- Scottish Mall Gurgaon
- Ansal Plaza Palam Vihar, Gurgaon
- House2Home Gurgaon
- Omaxe Plaza Gurgaon
- Gurgaon Mall Gurgaon
- Gurgaon Central
- First India Place
- Regent Square
- Regent Place
- Regent Plaza
- MGF SEL
- Regent Arcarde
- Shipul Agora
- Landmark Mall
- DLF South Point mall
- MGF Metropolis mall
- Raheja Shopping mall
- Regent Square mall
- Amusement mall
- Centre Plaza mall
- Vyapaar Kendra, Shushant Lok, Gurgaon.
- Shipul Agora

Noida

- The Centrestage Mall, Sector 18

- The Great India Place
- Sab Mall, Sector 27
- DLF Town Square Mall, Sector 18
- Garden Galleria
- Mall Eighteen, Sector 18
- Senior Mall, Sector 32
- Spice World Mall, Sector 25A
- Supertech Shopprix Mall, Sector 61.

DELHI ECONOMY

With an estimated net State Domestic Product (FY 2007) of Rs. 1,182 billion (US$24.5 billion) in nominal terms and Rs. 3,364 billion (US$69.8 billion) in PPP terms,Delhi is the largest commercial center in northern India. In 2007, Delhi had a per capita income of Rs. 66,728 (US$1,450) at current prices, the third highest in India after Chandigarh and Goa as of 2006-07. The tertiary sector contributes 70.95% of Delhi's gross SDP followed by secondary and primary sectors with 25.2% and 3.85% contribution respectively. Delhi's workforce constitutes 32.8% of the population showing an increase of 52.52% between 1991 and 2001. Delhi's unemployment rate decreased from 12.57% in 1999–2000 to 4.63% in 2003. In December 2004, 636,000 people were registered with various employment exchange programmes in Delhi.

In 2001 the total workforce in all government (union and state) and quasi-government sector was 620,000. In comparison, the organised private sector employed 219,000. Key service industries include information technology, telecommunications, hotels, banking, media and tourism. Delhi's manufacturing industry has also grown considerably as many consumer goods industries have established manufacturing units and headquarters in and around Delhi. Delhi's large consumer market, coupled with the easy availability of skilled labour, has attracted foreign investment in Delhi. In 2001, the manufacturing sector employed 1,440,000 workers while the number of industrial units was 129,000. Construction, power, telecommunications, health and community services, and real estate form integral parts of Delhi's economy. Delhi has India's largest and one of the fastest growing retail industries. As a result, land prices are booming and Delhi is currently ranked the 7th most expensive office hotspot in the world, with prices at $145.16 per square foot. As in the rest of India, the fast growth of retail is expected to affect the traditional unorganized retail trading system.

UTILITY SERVICES

The water supply in Delhi is managed by the Delhi Jal Board (DJB). As of 2006, it supplied 650 MGD (million gallons per day) of water, while the water demand for 2005–06 was estimated to be 963 MGD. The rest of the demand is met by private and public tube wells and hand pumps. At 240 MGD, the Bhakra storage is the largest water source for DJB, followed by river Yamuna and Ganges. With falling groundwater level and rising population density, Delhi faces severely acute water shortage. Delhi daily produces 8000 tonnes of solid wastes which is dumped at three landfill sites by MCD. The daily domestic waste water production is 470 MGD and industrial waste water is 70 MGD. A large portion of the sewerage flows untreated into the river Yamuna.

The city's per capita electricity consumption is about 1,265 kWh but actual demand is much more. In 1997,

Delhi Vidyut Board (DVB) replaced Delhi Electric Supply Undertaking which was managed by the MCD. The DVB itself cannot generate adequate power to meet the city's demand and borrows power from India's Northern Region Grid. As a result, Delhi faces a power shortage resulting in frequent blackouts and brownouts, especially during the summer season when energy demand is at its peak. Several industrial units in Delhi rely on their own electrical generators to meet their electric demand and for back up during Delhi's frequent and disruptive power cuts. A few years ago, the power sector in Delhi was handed over to private companies. The distribution of electricity is carried out by companies run by Tata Power and Reliance Energy. The Delhi Fire Service runs 43 fire stations that attend about 15,000 fire and rescue calls per year.

State-owned Mahanagar Telephone Nigam Limited (MTNL) and private enterprises like Vodafone Essar, Airtel, Idea cellular, Reliance Infocomm, and Tata Indicom provide telephone and cell phone service to the city. In May 2008, Airtel alone had approximately 4 million cellular subscribers in Delhi. Cellular coverage is extensive, and both GSM and CDMA (from Reliance and Tata Indicom) services are available. Affordable broadband internet penetration is increasing in the city.

MOTHER DAIRY

Mother Dairy, set up in 1974, is a wholly owned subsidiary of National Dairy Development Board (NDDB) of India.

Mother Dairy's range of products include the brands Mother Dairy (milk, milk products, curd, ice cream, butter, etc), Dhara (range of edible oils) and Safal (range of fresh fruits and vegetables, frozen vegetables, fruit juices). Mother Dairy Fruit and Vegetable Pvt. Ltd. offers the following products: Mother Dairy markets dairy products like Liquid Milk, Ice Creams, Flavoured Milk, Dahi, Lassi, Mishti Doi, Ghee, White Butter, Table Butter, Cheese, UHT Milk, Dhara range of edible oils and the Safal range of fresh Fruits & Vegetables, Frozen Vegetables and Fruit Juices at a national level, through its sales and distribution networks, for marketing food items. Mother Dairy milk (Bulk Vended Milk) is fortified with vitamin A @2000 IU per litre of milk as a part of social accountability. This program was started with the Mother Dairy, Delhi, since February 1980and there after Mother Dairy is continuing this program on their own as a social responsibility without having any financial assistance from the Government as well as since it is felt that BVM is generally consumed by the middle / lower middle / poor strata of the society. It is also found that the dietary practices adopted by these classes are deficient in Vitamin A. Mother Dairy sources significant part of its requirement of liquid milk from dairy cooperatives. Mother Dairy sources fruits and vegetables from farmers / growers associations. Mother Dairy also contributes to the cause of oilseeds grower cooperatives that manufacture/ pack the Dhara range of edible oils by undertaking to nationally market all Dhara products.

At Mother Dairy, processing of milk is controlled by process automation whereby state-of-the-art microprocessor technology is adopted to integrate and completely automate all functions of the milk processing areas to ensure high product quality/ reliability and safety. Mother Dairy is an IS/ ISO-9002, IS-15000 HACCP and IS-14001 EMS certified organization. Moreover, its Quality Assurance Laboratory is certified by National Accreditation Board for Testing and Calibration Laboratory (NABL)-Department of Science and Technology, Government of India.

Mother Dairy markets approximately 2.8 million liters of milk daily in the markets of Delhi, Mumbai, Saurashtra and Hyderabad. Mother Dairy Milk has a market share of 66% in the branded sector in Delhi where it sells 2.3 million liters of milk daily and undertakes its marketing operations through around 14,000 retail outlets and 845 exclusive outlets of Mother Dairy. The company's derives significant competitive advantage from its unique distribution network of bulk vending booths, retail outlets and mobile units. Mother Dairy ice creams launched in the year 1995 have shown continuous growth over the years and today boasts of approximately 62% market share in Delhi and NCR. Mother Dairy also manufactures and markets a wide range of dairy products that include Butter, Dahi, Ghee, Cheese, UHT Milk, Lassi & Flavored Milk and most of these products are available across the country. The company markets an array of fresh and frozen fruit and vegetable products under the brand name SAFAL through a chain of 400+ own Fruit and Vegetable shops and more than 20,000 retail outlets in various parts of the country. Fresh produce from the producers is handled at the Company's modern distribution facility in Delhi with an annual capacity of 200,000 MT.

An IQF facility with capacity of around 75 MT per day is also operational in Delhi. A state-of-the-art fruit processing plant of fruit handling capacity of 120 MT per day, a 100 percent EOU, setup in 1996 at Mumbai supplies quality products in the international market. With increasing demand another state-of-the-art fruit processing plant has been set up at Bangalore with fruit handling capacity of around 250 MT per day.

Quality Standards

Mother Dairy is an IS/ ISO 9002, IS 15000 HACCP

and IS 14001 EMS certified organization. Mother Dairy, Delhi has been awarded ISO 9001:2000 (Quality Management Systems), HACCP, 2002 RvA (Food Safety Management Systems) and ISO 14001:2004 (Environmental Management Systems) Certifications. Moreover, National Accreditation Board accredits its Quality Assurance Laboratory as per ISO/IEC 17025:1999 for Testing and Calibration Laboratories, Department of Science and Technology, Government of India.

DELHI VIDYUT BOARD

The Delhi Vidyut Board was formed by the Government of NCT Delhi in 1997 for the purpose of generation and distribution of power to the entire area of NCT of Delhi except the areas falling within the jurisdiction of NDMC and Delhi Cantonment Board. On July 1, 2002,The Delhi Vidyut Board (DVB) was unbundled into six successor companies: Delhi Power Supply Company Limited (DPCL)-Holding Company; Delhi Transco Limited (DTL) - TRANSCO; Indraprastha Power Generation Company Limited (IPGCL) - GENCO; BSES Rajdhani Power Limited (BRPL) - DISCOM; BSES Yamuna Power Limited (BYPL) - DISCOM; North Delhi Power Limited (NDPL) - DISCOM.

The position is that as per available records, the first diesel Power Station was established in Delhi in the year 1905 when a private English Company by name M/s. John Fleming was given permission to generate electricity under the provisions of the Indian Electricity Act 1903. The above mentioned Company was given the responsibility both of generation and distribution of power in a limited manner. That Company after obtaining license under the provisions of Electricity Act 1903 had set up a small 2 MW Diesel set at Lahori Gate in Old Delhi. Later on, this very Company was converted as Delhi Electricity Supply and Traction Company. In the Year 1911, the power generation was augmented by Steam Generation Station. In the year 1932, the management of Central Power House was handed over to New Delhi Municipal Committee (NDMC). In the field of power generation and distribution, a major break through was achieved in 1939 when Delhi Central Electricity Power Authority (DCEPA) was established. This Company was responsible for the supply of power to the areas covered by Local Bodies, namely, the Municipal Committees of Delhi, West Delhi and South Delhi, the Notified Area Committees of Red fort, Civil Lines, Mehrauli, Najaf Garh, amd the District Board of Delhi. The supply of electricity to the Municipal Committees of Delhi-Shahdara and the Notified Area of Narela was done by different private agencies. In 1947 DCEPA took over a Private Limited Company by name Delhi electric Supply & traction Company Limited.

In the year 1951 the Delhi State Electricity Board (DSEB) came into existence and the responsibility of generation and distribution of electricity was taken over by DSEB from DCEPA.

After the promulgation of the Delhi Municipal Corporation Act 1957, the DSEB was dissolved and the functions of DSEB were taken over by Delhi Electric Supply Undertaking (DESU), which came into existence in 1958. After the formation DESU, the generation and distribution of electricity to all the areas of Delhi came under DESU.

Formation of Delhi Vidyut Board (DVB)

The Government of the National Capital Territory of Delhi vide notification No. F.11 (10)/92-LSG /PF (II) dated 24.02.1997, issued under the Electricity (Supply) Act, 1948, constituted a separate Electricity Board, i.e. the Delhi

Vidyut Board (DVB) for the NCT of Delhi w.e.f. 24.02.1997 for the purpose of generation and distribution of power to the entire area of NCT of Delhi except the areas falling within the jurisdiction of NDMC and Delhi Cantonment Board.

The power situation in Delhi till a few year ago was yet another example of man's incapacity to handle another form of energy. The Delhi Vidyut Board (DVB) was a State Electricity Board set up in 1997 under the Electricity (Supply) Act, 1948, succeeding the Delhi Electricity Supply Undertaking (DESU) which has existed since 1957 as a wing of the Municipal Corporation of Delhi. It was an integrated utility with generation, transmission and distribution functions serving all of Delhi except the NDMC and MES (Cantoment) areas to which it supplied power in bulk.

The creation of DVB, replacing DESU, is 1997 proved to be merely a change in the legal status of the organization and was not followed by any real change in its structure, functioning and work culture. Its reputation continued to deteriorate and its poor commercial performance, the best known thing about DVB perhaps being its high Transmission and Distribution (T&D) losses made it a drain on the public exchequer. Further, failure in raising the resources necessary for improvement of its services made matters critical. There were unprecedented, widespread expressions of public discontent during the difficult summer of 1998.

In December 1998 when the present government came to power in Delhi, the power situation was grim to say the least. With T & D losses as high as 50% regular power cute for 10 to 15 hours and Delhi Vidyut board accumulating liabilities of over Rs. 23,000 crores, Delhi government had to come up with a fast and viable alternative. An alternative that would not only meet people's aspirations in terms of its end result but also be interesting enough for investors. And thus began a step by step process of a never-before fundamental power reform.

Delhi Electricity Board Regulatory Commission (DERC) was constituted in May 1999 whose prime responsibility was to look into the entire gamut of existing activity and search for various ways of power sector reforms. The DERC is even today a fully functional body which has since issued tariff orders for annual revenue requirement. Delhi Electricity Reform Ordinance, 2000 was a body which was promulgated in October 2000 and notified in the form of an Act in March 2001.

It mainly provides for the constitution of an Electricity Regulatory Commission, unbundling of DVB into separate generation, transmission and distribution companies and increasing avenues for participation of private sector. This was followed with a Tripartite Agreement which was signed by the government of Delhi, DVB employees to ensure the cooperation of stakeholders in this reform process. The tripartite agreement sent off very positive vibes to the people in general as well as to the investor community about the sincere and hassle-free objectives of power reforms.

Next, a two stage competitive bidding process of Request for Qualification (RFQ) and Request for Proposal (RFP) was set into motion for privatization of the distribution companies.

The bidders were selected on the basis of reduction of total Aggregate Technical and Commercial of losses (AT & C) a unique feature of the power sector reforms in Delhi. The bidders were required to bid on the basis of efficiency improvement like reduction of AT & C losses that they achieve year wise over a period of five years.

Despite privatisation, the electricity is still a big problem in Delhi. Frequent power cuts, indifferent attitude of provide companies etc. bring us to face a difficult time in Delhi. Perhaps a vicious nexus of vested interests is responsible for neglecting civic amenities in the city.

INDIRA GANDHI INTERNATIONAL AIRPORT

Indira Gandhi International Airport is an airport located in West Delhi, India. Named after former Prime Minister of India Indira Gandhi, it is the busiest airport in South Asia.It along with Mumbai's Chhatrapati Shivaji International Airport, handles more than half of the air traffic in South Asia. The airport serves as the primary civilian aviation hub for the National Capital Region of India. The airport was previously operated by the Indian Air Force until its management was transferred to the Airport Authority of India. In May 2006, the management of the airport was passed over to Delhi International Airport Limited (DIAL), a joint venture led by the GMR Group, which also has the responsibility for the airport's ongoing expansion and modernisation.

In 2007, the airport handled 23 million passengers annually and the planned expansion program will increase its capacity to handle 100 million passengers by 2030. The new Terminal 3 building, currently under construction and expected to cost US$2.6 billion, will have capacity to handle an additional 33 million passengers annually by the start of the 2010 Commonwealth Games. On completion, Indira Gandhi's Terminal 3 will become the world's third largest passenger terminal, after Dubai International Airport's Terminal 3 and Beijing International Airport's

Terminal 3. In September 2008, the airport inaugurated a 4.43 kilometre-long runway. Indira Gandhi International Airport (IGIA) was conferred the fourth best airport award in the world (in the 15-25 million category) and 'Best Improved Airport' in the Asia Pacific Region by Airport Council International.

The airport, earlier known as Palam Airport, was built around the second world war and served as an Air Force Station for the Indian Air Force. Passenger operations were later shifted to the airport from Safdarjung Airport in 1962 due to an increase in traffic. Palam Airport had a peak capacity of around 1300 passengers per hour.

Owing to an increase in air traffic in the 70s, an additional terminal with nearly four times the area of the old Palam terminal was constructed. With the inauguration of a new international terminal (Terminal 2), on 2 May 1986, the airport was renamed as Indira Gandhi International (IGI) Airport.

The old Palam terminal is now known as Terminal 1 and handles all domestic flights. The terminal is divided into three separate terminals - 1A (for domestic flights of state owned Indian Airlines, MDLR and Go Air), 1B (was used by other domestic airlines, now closed and demolished), the Domestic Arrival Terminal (1C) and the newly-constructed 1D (now used by all remaining domestic airlines). There is also a separate Technical Area for VVIP passengers. Additionally there is a separate terminal for Hajj flights.

Owing to the booming Indian Aviation industry and the entry of numerous low-cost private carriers, the airport saw a huge jump in passenger traffic and has failed to cope with the demand. The capacity of Terminal 1 is estimated to be 7.15 million passengers per annum (mppa). However, the actual throughput for 2005/06 was an estimated 10.4 million passengers. Including the international terminal (Terminal 2), the airport has a total capacity of 12.5 million passengers per year, whereas the total passenger traffic in 2006/07 was 16.5 million passengers per year In 2008, total passenger count at the airport reached 23.97 million.

Delhi Airport has two parallel runways and a non-parallel runway: Runway 11/29 (14,534 ft (4430m)) with CAT IIIB ILS on both sides and the main runway 10/28 (12,500 ft (3,810 m)) as well as an auxiliary runway 09/27 (9,229 ft (2,813 m)). Runway 10/28 and Runway 11/29 are the only two in South Asia to have been equipped with the CAT III-B instrument landing system. In the winter of 2005 there were a record number of disruptions at Delhi airport due to fog/smog. Since then some domestic airlines have trained their pilots to operate under CAT-II conditions of a minimum 350 m (1,150 ft) visibility. On 31 March 2006, IGI became the first Indian airport to operate two runways simultaneously following a test run involving a SpiceJet plane landing and a Jet Airways plane taking off at the same time.

In September 2008, the airport inaugurated a 4.43 kilometre long runway, making it one of the longest operational runways in Asia. The runway will increase the airport's capacity to handle 70 flights from the present 34-40 flights per hour. As of September 2008, the new runway was undergoing trials.

Terminals

IGI Airport is the home of several Indian airlines including Air India, Air India Regional, Indian Airlines, IndiGo, JetLite, SpiceJet. Jet Airways, Kingfisher Airlines, GoAir use IGI Airport as their secondary hub. Approximately

60 airlines serve this airport. There are Six operational terminals making up this airport, they are the following:

Terminal 1 - Domestic

Terminal 1A

Terminal 1A caters to all domestic flights operated by GoAir, MDLR, Indian Airlines and Air India Regional. This terminal was built in the early 90's to cater to Indian Airlines domestic flights only. It had to be refurbished after a fire gutted the interiors. DIAL, the owner of the airport, has significantly upgraded this terminal. It now sports a new look with modern washrooms and facilities, however will be torn down on the completion of newer terminals which are expected to finish construction in the coming years.

Terminal 1B

Terminal 1B has been closed for operations after the opening up of Terminal 1D which opened in April 2009.

Terminal 1C

The terminal in which all domestic operations (airlines from terminals 1A and 1D) arrive. The terminal is compact, however has received a new greeting area with expanded space, and a bigger luggage reclaim area.

Terminal 1D

Terminal 1D is the brand new interim domestic terminal, that was inaugurated on 26 February 2009. All domestic flights were moved to this new building from the second week of April, 2009. It is almost double the size of the current Terminal 1B. Once the new Terminal 3 is constructed in 2010, this terminal will be made solely to cater to the low cost carriers as the full fare airlines will also move to

Terminal 3, along with the international flights. Terminal 1D has the capacity to handle 10 million passengers per year.

Terminal 1D commenced operations on 15 April 2009. It is currently is used by IndiGo, Jet Airways, JetLite, Kingfisher Airlines and SpiceJet.

Terminal 2 - International

This terminal handles all international operations at the airport. However, constructed in the 80's, it is also in desperate need of repair, and it is half its size to cater to all its passengers. This sign of distress has already been taken care of. The entire terminal has been upgraded. It has been repainted,glass windows have replaced the old dark ones, floors have been refitted with tiles, walls and ceilings now have new surfaces, more immigration and emigration counters have been implemented, new seats have been brought in, new baggage belts, more business lounges, eateries, and duty free shops have also been added. Once all airlines move to the new Terminal 3 upon its completion in 2010 Terminal 2 will work in tandem with T3, until the proposed T4 terminal is built, upon which it will be demolished as per the proposed master plan.

Terminal 3

The state-of-the-art integrated terminal, called T3, of Indira Gandhi International Airport (IGIA) in New Delhi is poised to be the world's third-largest, after Dubai in the United Arab Emirates and Beijing in China, in terms of size. Once T3 starts operations before the 2010 Commonwealth Games in October, IGIA will become the world's sixth-largest in terms of capacity. T3 would increase the capacity of IGIA to 60 million passengers annually, from 23 million after it starts commercial operation in July 2010.

Designed by HOK working in consultation with Mott MacDonald, the new Terminal 3 will be a two-tier building, with the bottom floor being the arrivals area, and the top being a departures area. This terminal will have 168 check-in counters, 74 aerobridges, 30 parking bays, 72 immigration counters, 15 X-ray screening areas, for less waiting times, duty-free shops, and other features. Over 90% of passengers will use this terminal when completed. This new terminal has been completed in time for the 2010 Commonwealth Games, which are to be held in Delhi, and will be connected to Delhi by an eight-lane motorway (National Highway 8), and the Delhi Mass Rapid Transit System. Terminal 3 will cater to more than 35 million passengers a year.

The new integrated terminal 3 (T3) with a capacity of 34 million passengers per annum will become operational from July 3 after which all international airlines and India's full cost carriers Air India, Jet Airways and Kingfisher Airlines will start their operations from the terminal in a phased manner. Members of the Oneworld alliance will also operate from this terminal as a result of Kingfisher Airlines's entry into the alliance.

Terminal 3 will form the first phase of the airport expansion in which a 'U' shaped building will be developed in a modular manner. In 2010, all international and full service domestic carriers will operate from Terminal 3, while Terminal 1 will be dedicated to low cost operations. In subsequent stages, the low cost carriers will also move to the new terminal complex.

Terminal 4 and 5

Terminal 4 and 5 will be built at a later stage,which

will be triggered by growth in traffic, and once completed, all international flights will move to these two new terminals, while Terminal 3 will then solely be used for handling domestic air traffic. A new cargo handling building is also planned. According to Delhi International Airport Limited (DIAL), these new terminals will cost approximately US$7.5 billion dollars and will increase the airport's annual passenger volume capacity to 100 million.

Hajj Terminal

Upon the annual Muslim pilgrimage of Hajj, all airlines bound for the Middle East move to this separate terminal to prevent disruption of other passengers who are traveling to other areas of the globe. A separate area has been made for Hajj to cater to the abundance of additional travelers during this season, and to accommodate them with enough provided space. It has a 10 million passengers per year capacity. It is used from October to December. Plans are underway to use the building for the remaining 10 months of the year also.

Cargo Terminal

The Cargo Terminal handles all cargo operations. The airport received an award in 2007 for its excellent and organised cargo handling system.

Ground Transportation

Connected from Delhi by the Delhi Gurgaon Expressway. Low floor buses regularly run between the airport and the city. Delhi Metro link to be completed by 2010. DTC operates several buses to the airport.

The Delhi Metro is currently constructing an "Airport Express" metro line connecting the airport to New Delhi, which is planned to be completed by 2010.

Prepaid taxis are also available from the terminal to all areas of Delhi.

Fixed Base Operators (FBO)

Caterers

- Ambassador's SkyChef
- Chef Air
- Taj-Sats
- Oberoi Flight Services
- Sky Gourmet Catering Pvt Ltd

Fuelers

- Bharat Petroleum
- Hindustan Petroleum
- Indian Oil Corporation

Ground Handlers

- NACIL
- GlobeGround India
- Airworks India
- Cambata Aviation
- Livewel Aviation Services Pvt Ltd.
- Concord Aviation Pvt Ltd.

DELHI TOURISM AND TRANSPORTATION DEVELOPMENT CORPORATION

Delhi Tourism and Transportation Development Corporation (DTTDC) is an undertaking of the Government of Delhi, India, that was established in December 1975 for the purpose of promoting tourism and related services in the city of

Delhi. It has an authorized share capital of Rs. 10.00 crores and a paid up capital of Rs. 6.28 crores. It is involved in several other activities, some of which do not fall under the core activity of promotion of tourism, such as the selling of liquor. This particular activity, however, provides the corporation with revenue that can be utilized in tourism or other related development activities for the National Capital Region of Delhi.

Main Activities

The main activities of Delhi Tourism can be divided into the following heads.

Publicity Literature

The Corporation promotes tourism whether or not the activities provide any short-term benefits in terms of revenue. The gains from the promotion of these activities is reviewed regularly as part of a longer term strategy. The use of published literature for publicity and the promotion of tourism is limited to the publication of the following:

- Tourism Map of Delhi
- Eicher City Guide
- CD-ROM on Delhi to provide vital information for the tourist
- Annual Calendar and Diary
- First Mini Booklet for Distribution in inbound flight

Tourist Facilitation

A large number of tourists arrive at the capital of Delhi every year. Activities provided to tourists regarding include:

- Package Tours - limited to very few choices, or sometimes to only one destination.
- Travel Services - travel services in the form of international air ticketing and foreign exchange banking.
- Tourist Transport - taxi services are also provided by the transport division.

Other Tourist Activities

The Corporation provides several other activities for tourists. They are:

- Azad Hind Gram - a rural tourist complex with amphitheater and a museum in the memory of the freedom fighter Subhash Chandra Bose
- four Coffee Homes - run by the Catering Division of DTTDC are located at prime locations in Delhi.
- Dilli Haat - a market providing items for sale directly by the craftsmen from different parts of the country at one place, recognized as an art, crafts and cultural centre of Delhi, which was visited by approximately 16 lakhs visitors in 2001.
- Exhibition and Conference
- Musical Fountain - located at Ajmal Khan Park with water cascades synchronized to coloured lights, each show lasts 20 minutes.
- Sound and Light show (Son-et-lumiere) - takes place at the Old Fort and projects the Fort's history realistically through weekly one hour shows in Hindi and English covering the history of Delhi over a period of 5000 years.

Other activities include boating at nearby lakes and arranging for parasailing and mountaineering activities in India.

Selling of Liquor

Besides the core activity of promotion of tourism, the Corporation directly sells liquor all over Delhi, which is one of the few activities that provides net profit to the corporation. The sale of liquor is carried out through liquor shops, which number over one hundred, and includes the direct selling of Indian Made Foreign Liquor (IMFL) and Country Made Liquor (CL).

Infrastructure

The Corporation constructs flyovers as part of the development of infrastructure for easy commuting by tourists in Delhi. The revenue for the construction of some of the flyovers in Delhi has been generated from a share of profit that the Corporation earns from the sale of Country made Liquor (CL). The Corporation charges a flat rate of profit, a margin of Rs.6 per bottle of country liquor, of which a share of Rs.5/- has been fixed as a contribution towards the construction of flyovers. The construction is carried out by the Engineering Division of the Corporation.

Indian Institute of Tourism and Travel Management

The Indian Institute of Tourism and Travel Management (Delhi Chapter) provides short-term diploma programmes in Tourism and Travel Management on a continuous basis, which assists development of tourism by transferring knowledge in areas of tour and tourism.

Proposed Projects

DTTDC has several projects planned:

- Garden of Five Senses, Said-ul-Aj-Ajaib
- Development of Four Dilli Haats.
- Water Sports Tourism Complex at Bhaalswa Lake
- Establishment of Wayside Amenities at N.H.-8.
- Development of a Mini India Heritage Complex
- Restoration of denotified monuments
- Refurbishment of monuments
- Tourist reception centers
- Meet and Assist Services
- Radio Cabs
- Photo Identity Cards .
- Illumination of Monuments
- Development of Lakes
- Use of Information Technology-Helpline/ call center
- 52 Episode tele-serial on tourism
- Handy Audio reach kit
- Computer kiosks with WLL phones.

SALAAM BAALAK CITY WALK – NEW DELHI

The Salaam City Walk is a guided tour around New Delhi Railway Station and Paharganj area in which former street children share their personal story of survival with the participants and show them the contact points and shelter homes Salaam Baalak Trust provides.

Since about three years it is run by Salaam Baalak Trust (SBT) - a non-profit organization, taking care of street- and former street-children in Delhi. Through this program the young guides get an opportunity to improve their communication and marketing skills independently.

The Walk aims to sensitize people to the lives of street children and helps to provide a deeper insight about street life from people who have experienced it themselves.

Often people who are coming to Delhi from Europe or the Western World don't get in touch with poverty and the real problems Indian society is facing. During the Walk the participants get to know another side of Delhi:

- why children run away from home,
- how they learn to survive on the street,
- how they even enjoy their life on the street because they are independent, and
- how eventually they can choose their future over this freedom.

Some of the children have taken the opportunity to change their lives and now they are going to university, studying different languages, working as professional photographers or for example as tour guide for The Walk.

All proceeds go directly to the trust to enable more opportunities to be made for street children -so the walk is 100% non-profit making.

7

Tourism and Major Tourist Attactions

Being one of the most historic capitals in the world, Delhi has many tourist sites. This is a list of Delhi's tourist sites.

In Old Delhi, there are attractions like mosques, forts and other monuments that represent India's history. The important places in Old Delhi include the majestic Red Fort. New Delhi, on the other hand, is a modern city designed by Edwin Lutyens and Herbert Baker. New Delhi houses many government buildings and embassies, apart from places of historical interest.

The Qutub Minar, Red Fort and Humayun's Tomb have been declared World Heritage Sites.

Rashtrapati Bhawan

Built with a mix of Western and Indian styles, Rashtrapati Bhavan was originally built for the Governor General of India. Inaugurated in 1931 as the Viceregal Lodge, the name was changed in 1950 after India became a republic. Now it is the Presidential Palace of India.

India Gate and Rajpath

Situated along the ceremonial Rajpath avenue (meaning King's Way) in New Delhi, India Gate is a memorial raised in honour of the Indian soldiers who died during the Afghan wars and World War I. The names of the soldiers who died in these wars are inscribed on the walls. The cenotaph (or shrine) in the middle is constructed with black marble and depicts a rifle placed on its barrel, crested by a soldier's helmet. Each face of the cenotaph has inscribed in gold the words *Amar Jawan* (in Hindi, meaning Immortal Warrior). The green lawns at India Gate are a popular evening and holiday rendezvous for young and old alike.

Laxminarayan Temple

Also called the Birla Mandir, the Laxminarayan Temple was built by the Birla family in 1938. Along with the temple itself, the name 'Laxminarayan Temple' encompasses a large garden with fountains behind it. The temple attracts thousands of devotees on Janmashtami day, the birthday of Lord Krishna.

Akshardham Temple

Akshardham Temple it is the largest Hindu temple in the world. In the sprawling 100-acre (0.40 km^2) land rests an intricately carved monument, high-technology exhibitions, an IMAX theatre, a musical fountain, a food court and gardens.

Gurdwara Bangla Sahib

One of the many Gurdwaras in Delhi, Gurdwara Bangla Sahib is the most visited one in the Delhi area. Millions visit this Gurdwara from all over the world and of all religions to offer their prayers at this elegant yet historical Gurdwara in Delhi. This is not just a sacred Sikh shrine, but also very important to many Hindus .

Humayun's Tomb

Humayun's Tomb was built by Humayun's widow, Hamida Banu Begum. Designed by a Persian architect named Mirak Mirza Ghiyas, the structure was begun in 1562 and completed in 1565. The tomb established a standard for all later Mughal monuments, which followed its design, most notably the Taj Mahal.

Qutub Minar

The Qutub Minar is located in a Mehrauli in South Delhi. It was built by Qutb-ud-din Aibak of the Slave Dynasty, who took possession of Delhi in 1206. It is a fluted red sandstone tower, which tapers up to a height of 72.5 metres and is covered with intricate carvings and verses from the Qur'an. Qutub-ud-din Aybak began constructing this victory tower as a sign of Muslim domination of Delhi and as a minaret for the muezzin to call the faithful to prayer. However, only the first story was completed by Qutub-ud-din. The other stories were built by his successor Iltutmish. The two circular stories in white marble were built by Ferozshah Tughlaq in 1368, replacing the original fourth story.

The balconies in the tower are supported by exquisite stalactite designs. The tapering tower has pointed and circular flutings on the first storey and star-shaped ones on the second and third stories.

The Qutub Minar is also significant for what it represents in the history of Indian culture. In many ways, the Qutub Minar, the first monument built by a Muslim ruler in India, heralded the beginning of a new style of art and architecture that came to be known as the Indo-Islamic style. Other monuments around the Qutb complex, are

Jamaali Kamaali mosque and tombs, Balban's tomb and Adham Khan's Tomb.

Red Fort

The decision for constructing the Red Fort was made in 1639, when Shah Jahan decided to shift his capital from Agra to Delhi. Within eight years, Shahjahanabad was completed with the Red Fort-Qila-i-Mubarak (fortunate citadel) — Delhi's seventh fort — ready in all its magnificence to receive the Emperor. Though much has changed with the large-scale demolitions during the British occupation of the fort, its important structures have survived.

Salimgarh Fort

Salimgarh Fort, which is now part of the Red Fort complex, was constructed on an island of the Yamuna River in 1546. But a gate called the Bahadur Shahi Gate for entry into the Fort from the northern side was constructed only in 1854-55 by Bahadur Shah Zafar, the last Mogul ruler of India. The gate was built in brick masonry with moderate use of red sandstone. The fort was used during the Uprising in 1857 and also as a prison which housed Zebunnisa daughter of Aurangzeb and the British imprisoned the freedom fighters of the INA. The layout of the Red Fort was organized to retain and integrate this site with the Salimgarh Fort through the Bahadur Shah Gate. The fort has been renamed as Swatantrata Senani Smarak and a plaque at the entrance to the fort attests to this.

Chandni Chowk

Chandni Chowk, a main marketplace in Delhi, keeps alive the city's living legacy of Shahjahanabad. Created by Shah Jahan the builder of Taj Mahal, the old city, with the Red Fort as its focal point and Jama Masjid as the praying centre, has a fascinating market called Chandnı Chowk. Legend has it that Shah Jahan planned Chandni Chowk so that his daughter could shop for all that she wanted. The market was divided by canals. The canals are now closed, but Chandni Chowk remains Asia's largest wholesale market. Crafts once patronized by the Mughals continue to flourish there. Chowk is one of the oldest and busiest markets in central north Delhi. the Laal Quila (The Red Fort) and Fateh Puri Masjid. With the most famous mosque of Delhi Jama Masjid in the vicinity, along with Sis Ganj Gurudwara, Jain Mandir and a lot of small temples, the place witnesses a genuine cultural harmony.

Jama Masjid

The Masjid-i-Jahan Numa, commonly known as Jama Masjid, is the principal mosque of Old Delhi. Commissioned by the Mughal Emperor Shah Jahan and completed in the year 1656, it is one of the largest and best known mosques in India.

Raj Ghat

On the bank Yamuna River, which flows past Delhi, there is Raj Ghat, the final resting place of Mahatma Gandhi, the father of the nation. It has become an essential point of call for all visiting dignitaries. Two museums dedicated to Gandhi are situated nearby.

Shanti Van

Lying close to the Raj Ghat, the Shanti Vana (literally, the forest of peace) is the place where India's first Prime Minister Jawaharlal Nehru was cremated. The area is now a beautiful park adorned by trees planted by visiting dignitaries and heads of state.

Lotus Temple

The Lotus Temple is a Bahá'í House of Worship, situated in South Delhi and shaped like a lotus. It was built by the Bahá'í community.

Purana Quila

The Purana Quila (Old Fort) is a good example of medieval military architecture. Built by Humayun, with later modifications by Sher Shah Suri, the Purana Quila is a monument of bold design, which is strong, straightforward, and every inch a fortress. It is different from the well-planned, carefully decorated, and palatial forts of the later Mughal rulers. Purana Quila is also different from the later forts of the Mughals, as it does not have a complex of palaces, administrative, and recreational buildings as is generally found in the forts built later on. The main purpose of this now dilapidated fort was its utility with less emphasis on decoration. The Qal'a-I-Kunha Masjid and the Sher are two important monuments inside the fort. It was made by Aqeel in 1853.

Tughlaqabad

When Ghazi Malik founded the Tughlaq Dynasty in 1321, he built the strongest fort in Delhi at Tughlaqabad, completed with great speed within four years of his rule. It is said that Ghazi Malik, when only a slave to Mubarak Khilji, had suggested this rocky prominence as an ideal site for a fort. The Khilji Sultan laughed and suggested that the slave build a fort there when he became a Sultan. Ghazi Malik as Ghiyasuddin Tughlaq did just that: Tughlaqabad is Delhi's most colossal and awesome fort even in its ruined state. Within its sky-touching walls, double-storied bastions, and gigantic towers were housed grand palaces, splendid mosques, and audience halls.

Jantar Mantar

The Jantar Mantar consists of 13 architectural astronomy instruments, built by Maharaja Jai Singh II between 1727 to 1734.

Safdarjung's Tomb

The Safdarjung's Tomb is a garden tomb in a marble mausoleum.

Lodhi Gardens

The Lodhi Gardens is a park spread over 90 acres. It contains architectural works of the 15th century Sayyid and Lodhis, a Pathan dynasty which ruled much of Northern India during the 16th century.

Nizamuddin Dargah

Nizamuddin Dargah is the Mausoleum of the famous Sufi Saint Nizamuddin Auliya, Delhi.

Sansad Bhavan

Sansad Bhavan or the Parliament of India is a circular building designed by the British architects Sir Edwin Lutyens and Sir Herbert Baker in 1912–1913. Construction began in 1921, and in 1927 the building was opened as the home of the Council of State, the Central Legislative Assembly, and the Chamber of Princes.

National Museum, New Delhi

The National Museum, New Delhi is the largest museum in India. It holds variety of articles ranging from pre-historic era to modern works of art. It is run by the Ministry of Culture, part of the Government of India. The museum is situated on the corner of Janpath and Maulana Azad Road.

Now we will given an elaborate description of some select tourist attractions of Delhi, giving details of location, history etc.

National Zoological Park (Chiriaghar)

Delhi National Zoological Park is a zoo near the Old Fort in Delhi, India. It extends over 214 acres, and has more than 2,000 species of animals and birds belonging to many different places around the world.

The zoo can be seen on foot or using a battery-operated vehicle. Visitors are not permitted to bring any food other than drinking water, although there is a canteen in the zoo. The zoo is quite busy during on weekends, and in the heat of summer many animals prefer to rest during the day rather than being active so that visitors can see them.

Jantar Mantar

The Yantra Mantra (literally the 'instrument and formula' and often called the Jantar Mantar), is located in the modern city of New Delhi, Delhi. It consists of 13 architectural astronomy instruments, built by Maharaja Jai Singh II of Jaipur, from 1724 onwards, and is one of five built by him, as he was given by Mughal emperor Muhammad Shah the task of revising the calendar and astronomical tables. There is plaque fixed on one of the structures in the Jantar Mantar observatory in New Delhi that was placed there in 1910 mistakenly dating the construction of the complex to the year 1710. Later research, though, suggests 1724 as the actual year of construction.

The primary purpose of the observatory was to compile astronomical tables, and to predict the times and movements of the sun, moon and planets. Some of these purposes nowadays would be classified as astrology.

There are four distinct instruments within the observatory of Jantar Mantar in New Delhi: the Samrat Yantra, the Ram Yantra, the Jayaprakash, and the Mishra yantras.

- Samrat Yantra: The Samrat Yantra, or Supreme Instrument, is a giant triangle that is basically an equal hour sundial. It is 70 feet high, 114 feet long at the base, and 10 feet thick. It has a 128 foot long hypotenuse that is parallel to the Earth's axis and points toward the North Pole. On either side of the triangle is a quadrant with graduations indicating hours, minutes, and seconds. At the time of the Samrat Yantra's construction, sundials already existed, but the Samrat Yantra turned the basic sundial into a precision tool for measuring declination and other related coordinates of various heavenly bodies.
- Jayaprakash Yatra: The Jayaprakash consists of hollowed out hemispheres with markings on their concave surfaces. Crosswires were stretched between points on their rim. From inside the Ram, an observer could align the position of a star with various markings or a window's edge.
- Mishra Yantra: The Mishra yantras were able to indicate when it was noon in various cities all over the world and was the only structure in the observatory not invented by Jai Singh II.

In all, between 1727 and 1734, Jai Singh II, built five similar observatories, Yantra Mantras, in west central India, all known by the same name, thus includes ones at Jaipur -Yantra Mantra (Jaipur), Ujjain, Mathura and Varanasi. Today the observatory is mainly a tourist attraction, and is significant in the history of astronomy.

Safdarjung's Tomb

Safdarjung's Tomb is a garden tomb in a marble mausoleum in Delhi, India. It was built in 1754 in the style of late Mughal architecture. The top story of the edifice houses the Archaeological Survey of India. The garden, in the style evolved by the Mughal Empire that is now known as the Mughal gardens style known as a *charbagh*, is entered through an ornate gate. Its facade is decorated with elaborate plaster carvings.

The tomb was built for Safdarjung, the powerful prime minister of Muhammad Shah who was the weak Mughal emperor from 1719 to 1748. The central tomb has a huge dome. There are four water canals leading to four buildings. One has an ornately decorated gateway while the other three are pavilions, with living quarters built into the walls. Octagonal towers are in the corners. The canals are four oblong tanks, one on each side of the tomb.

Lodi Gardens

Lodi Gardens is a park in Delhi. Spread over 90 acres, it contains, Mohammed Shah's Tomb, Sikander Lodi's Tomb, Sheesh Gumbad and Bara Gumbad, architectural works of the 15th century Sayyid and Lodis, a Pashtun dynasty which ruled much of Northern India during the 16th century, and the site is now protected by Archeological Survey of India (ASI). The gardens are situated between Khan Market and Safdarjung's Tomb on Lodi Road. It is beautiful and serene, and is a hotspot for morning walks for the Delhiites.

The tomb of Mohammed Shah, the last of the Sayyid dynasty rulers, the earliest of the tombs in the garden, was built in 1444 by Ala-ud-din Alam Shah as a tribute to Mohammed Shah.

As there is little architecture from these two periods remaining in India, Lodi Gardens is an important place of preservation. The tomb of Mohammed Shah is visible from the road, and is the earliest structure in the gardens. The architecture is characterised by the octagonal chamber, with stone *chhajjas* on the roof and *guldastas* on the corners.

Another tomb within the gardens is that of Sikander Lodi, which is similar to Mohammed Shah's tomb, though without the *chhatris*, it was built by his son Ibrahim Lodi in 1517, the last of Sultan of Delhi from Lodi dynasty, as he was defeated by Babur, First battle of Panipat in 1526, this laying the foundation of the Mughal Empire. His tomb is often mistaken to be the *Sheesh Gumbad*, and is actually situated in near the tehsil office in Panipat, close to the Dargah of Sufi saint Bu Ali Shah Qalandar.

It is a simple rectangular structure on a high platform approached by a flight of steps. The tomb was renovated by the British, and an inscription mentioning Ibrahim Lodi's defeat at the hands of Babur and the renovation was included in 1866.

In the centuries, after the 15th century Sayyid and Lodi dynasties, two villages grew around the monuments, but the villagers were relocated in 1936 in order to create the gardens. During British Raj, it was landscaped by Lady Willingdon, wife of Governor-General of India, Marquess of Willingdon, and hence named the 'Lady Willingdon Park' upon its inauguration on April 9, 1936, and 1947, after Independence, it was given its present name, Lodi Gardens. Later, it was re-landscaped in 1968 by JA Stein, who also designed the adjacent India International Centre, along with Garrett Eckbo, during the time Stein also made a glass house within the park. A

British-period gateway, is still being used as an entrance that once welcomed visitors to 'Lady Willingdon Park'.

Raj Ghat

Raj Ghat is a memorial to Mahatma Gandhi, the father of nation. It is a black marble platform that marks the spot of Gandhi's cremation on 31 January 1948. It is left open to the sky while an eternal flame burns perpetually at one end. It is located on the banks of the river Yamuna in Delhi in India on Ring Road officially known as Mahatma Gandhi Road. A stone footpath flanked by lawns leads to the walled enclosure that houses the memorial. Two museums dedicated to Gandhi, including the National Gandhi Museum, are located near by.

The memorial has the epitaph *He Ram*, (literally 'O' Ram', but also translated to 'O God'), believed to be the last words uttered by Gandhi. The memorial was designed by Vanu G. Bhuta. It was originally designed to reflect the simplicity of Mahatma Gandhi's life. The design that won the government of India invitational competition had the black marble slab surrounded by red earth as none of Gandhiji's ashram residences had any "English lawn". The memorial has gone through a number of design changes since then, a few at the behest of Jawaharlal Nehru, the first Prime Minister of independent India.

In recent years, it has become customary for foreign dignitaries visiting India to pay their respects to Gandhi at the Raj Ghat by laying flowers or wreaths on the platform. As a sign of respect, visitors are required to remove footwear before approaching the memorial. A commemorative ceremony is held every Friday. Prayer sessions are held at the Raj Ghat on Gandhi's birth and death anniversaries.

Other Memorials

Raj Ghat loosely translates to *King's Bank* (where King alludes to the importance of the place and Bank as in -on the bank of river Yamuna). Several other *samâdhis* or cremation spots of other famous leaders can be found in the vicinity of Raj Ghat on the banks of the Yamuna. The landscaping and planting of these memorials was performed by Sydney Percy-Lancaster, the Secretary of the Agri Horticultural Society of India, and the last Englishman to hold the post of Superintendent of Horticultural Operations, Government of India.

Jawaharlal Nehru's samadhi is to the north of the Raj Ghat and is known as the Shantivan or Shanti Vana meaning the *forest of peace*. The area has a beautiful park adorned with trees planted by visiting dignitaries and heads of state. His grandson Sanjay Gandhi's samadhi is adjacent to it.

Qutb Minar

The Qutb Minar a tower in Delhi, India, is at 72.5 meters (237.8 ft) the world's tallest brick minaret. Construction commenced in 1193 under the orders of India's first Muslim ruler Qutb-ud-din Aibak, and the topmost storey of the minaret was completed in 1386 by Firuz Shah Tughluq. The Qutb Minar is notable for being one of the earliest and most prominent examples of Indo-Islamic architecture.

It is surrounded by several other ancient and medieval structures and ruins, collectively known as Qutb complex. The complex is listed as a UNESCO World Heritage Site. It is one of the most popular tourist destinations in Delhi, and was also India's most visited monument in 2006, as it attracted 3.9 million visitors, even more than the Taj Mahal, which drew about 2.5 million visitors

The Qutab Minar is tall, with 379 steps leading to the top. The diameter of the base is 14.3 meters, while the top floor measures 2.75 meters in diameter. Surrounding the building are many fine examples of Indian artwork from the time it was built in 1193. A second tower was in construction and planned to be taller than the Qutb Minar itself. Its construction ended abruptly when it was about 12 meters tall.The name of this tower is given as Alai Minar and construction of recent studies shows that this structure has been tilted in one direction. It is made of red sandstone all the way except for two stories at the top. This part is of white marble and was made by Firoz Shah Tughlaq. He had decided to put a prominent finish to the magnificent minar.

Inspired by the Minaret of Jam in Afghanistan and wishing to surpass it, Qutbuddin Aibak, the first Muslim ruler of Delhi, commenced construction of the Qutb Minar in 1193, but could only complete its base. His successor, Iltutmish, added three more stories and, in 1286, Ala-ud-din constructed the fifth and the last story. The development of architectural styles from Aibak to Tughluq is quite evident in the minaret. Like earlier towers erected by the Ghaznavids and Ghurids in Afghanistan, the Qutb Minar comprises several superposed flanged and cylindrical shafts, separated by balconies carried on Muqarnas corbels. The minaret is made of fluted red sandstone covered with intricate carvings and verses from the Qur'an.

The Qutb Minar is itself built on the ruins of the Lal Kot, the Red Citadel in the city of Dhillika, the capital of the Tomars and the Chauhans, the last Hindu rulers of Delhi. The complex initially housed 27 ancient Hindu and

Jain temples, which were destroyed and their debris used to build the Qutb minar. One engraving on the Qutb Minar reads, "Shri Vishwakarma prasade rachita" (*Conceived with the grace of Vishwakarma*). The purpose for building this monument has been variously speculated upon. It could take the usual role of a minaret, calling people for prayer in the Quwwat-ul-Islam mosque, the earliest extant mosque built by the Delhi Sultans. Other possibilities are a tower of victory, a monument signifying the might of Islam, or a watch tower for defense. Controversy also surrounds the origins for the name of the tower. Many historians believe that the Qutb Minar was named after the first Turkish sultan, Qutb-ud-din Aibak, but others contend that it was named in honour of Qutbuddin Bakhtiar Kaki, a saint from Transoxiana who came to live in India and was greatly venerated by Iltutmish.

The nearby Iron Pillar is one of the world's foremost metallurgical curiosities, standing in the famous Qutb complex. According to the traditional belief, anyone who can encircle the entire column with their arms, with their back towards the pillar, can have their wish granted. Because of the corrosive qualities of sweat the government has built a fence around it for safety.

The minar did receive some damage because of earthquakes on more than a couple of occasions but was reinstated and renovated by the respective rulers. During the rule of Firoz Shah, the minar's two top floors were damaged due to an earthquake but were repaired by Firoz Shah. In the year 1505, earthquake again struck and it was repaired by Sikandar Lodi. Later on in the year 1794, the minar faced another earthquake and it was Major Smith, an engineer who repaired the affected parts of the minar. He replaced Firoz Shah's pavilion with his own pavilion at the top. The pavilion was removed in the year 1848 by Lord Hardinge and now it can be seen between the Dak Bungalow and the Minar in the garden. The floors built by Firoz Shah can be distinguished easily as the pavilions was built of white marbles and are quite smooth as compared to other ones.

Qutb Complex

The *Qutb complex*, is an array of monuments and buildings at Mehrauli in Delhi, India, the most famous of which is the five-storeyed, and 72.5 m high Qutb Minar built in 1192 AD, by Qutbuddin Aibak, viceroy and general in Mohammed Ghori of Ghazni's army to mark their victory over Delhi. Qutbuddin later became the first ruler of the Slave Dynasty, and after his death the Minar was added upon by his successor Iltutmish (aka Altamash) and much later by Firoz Shah Tughlaq, a Tughlaq dynasty, Sultan of Delhi in 1368 AD. The complex initially housed a complex of twenty-seven ancient Jain temples which were destroyed and their material used in the construction of the Quwwat-ul-Islam Mosque next to the Qutb Minar, in the Qutb complex, built on the ruins of Lal Kot Fort built by Tomar Rajput ruler, Anangpal in 739 CE and Qila-Rai-Pithora, Prithviraj Chauhan's city, the Rajput king, whom Ghori's Afghan armies had earlier defeated and killed, at the Second Battle of Tarain.

The complex was added to by many subsequent rulers, including Firoz Shah Tughlaq and Ala ud din Khilji as well as the British.

The most famous monument situated in the complex is the Qutb Minar; other important constructions in the complex are the Quwwat ul-Islam Mosque, the Alai Gate, the Alai Minar, the Iron pillar, and the tombs of Iltutmish,

Alauddin Khilji and Imam Zamin; surrounded by Jain temple ruins.

Today, the adjoining area spread over 100 acres, with a host of old monuments, including Balban's tomb, has been developed by Archeological Survey of India (ASI) as the Mehrauli Archeological Park, and INTACH has restored some 40 monuments in the Park. It is also the venue of the annual 'Qutub Festival', held in November-December, where artists, musicians and dancers perform over three days. Qutb Minar complex, with 38.95 lakh visitors, was India's most visited monument in 2006, ahead of the Taj Mahal, which drew about 25.4 lakh visitors.

Alai Darwaza

The Alai Darwaza (*Alai Gate*) is the main gateway from southern side of the Quwwat-ul-Islam Mosque. It was built by the second Khilji Sultan of Delhi, Ala-ud-din Khilji in 1311 AD, who also added a court to the pillared to the eastern side. The domed gateway is decorated with red sandstone and inlaid white marble decorations, inscriptions in Naskh script, latticed stone screens and showcases the remarkable craftsmanship of the Turkish artisans who worked on it. This is the first building in India to employ Islamic architecture principles in its construction and ornamentation

The Slave dynasty did not employ true Islamic architecture styles and used false domes and false arches, this makes the Alai Darwaza, the earliest example of first true arches and true domes in India. It is considered to be one of the most important buildings built in the Delhi sultanate period. With its pointed arches and spearhead of fringes, identified as lotus buds, it adds grace to the Quwwat-ul-Islam mosque to which it served as an entrance.

The world famous Qutb Minar is also situated in this complex.. Qutb Minar is the tallest brick minaret in the world, inspired by the Minaret of Jam in Afghanistan, it is an important example of early Afghan architecture, which later evolved into Indo-Islamic Architecture. The Qutb Minar is 72.5 metres (239 ft) high, has five distinct storeys, each marked by a projecting balcony carried on muqarnas corbel and tapers from a diameter 14.3 metres at the base to 2.7 metres at the top, which is 379 steps away. It is listed as a UNESCO World Heritage Site along with surrounding buildings and monuments.

Built as a Victory Tower, to celebrate the the victory of Mohammed Ghori over Rajput king, Prithviraj Chauhan, in 1192 AD, by his then viceroy, Qutbuddin Aibak, later the first Sultan of Mamluk dynasty. Its construction also marked the end last of Hindu kingdoms in North India, and the beginning of Muslim rule in India, which ended only in the 19th century with the arrival of the British, and even today the Qutb remains one of the most important "Towers of Victory" in the Islamic world. Aibak however, could only build the first storey, for this reason the lower storey is replete with eulogies to Mohammed Ghori . The next three floors were added by his son-in-law and successor, Iltutmish. The minar was first struck by lightning in 1368 AD, which knocked off its top storey, after that it was replaced by the existing two floors by Firoz Shah Tughlaq, a later Sultan of Delhi 1351 to 1388, and faced with white marble and sandstone enhancing the distinctive variegated look of the minar, as seen in lower three storeys. Thus the structure displays a marked variation in architectural styles from Aibak to that of Tughlaq dynasty.

The minar made with numerous superimposed flanged and cylindrical shafts in the interior, and fluted columns on the exterior, which have a 40 cm thick veneer of red and buff coloured sandstone; all surrounded by bands of intricate carving in Kufic style of Islamic calligraphy, giving the minar the appearance of bundled reeds. It stands just outside the Quwwatul mosque, and an Arabic inscription suggests that it might have been built to serve as a place for the muezzin, to call the faithfuls for *namaz*. Also marking a progression in era, is the appearance of inscriptions in a bold and cursive Thuluth script of calligraphy on the Qutb Minar, distinguished by strokes that thicken on the top, as compared to Kufic in earlier part of the construction.

Inscriptions also indicate further repairs by Sultan Sikander Lodi in 1503, when it was struck by lightning once again. In 1803, the cupola on the top was thrown down and the whole pillar was damaged by an earthquake. It was repaired by Major R. Smith of the Royal Engineers who restored the Qutub Minar in 1829 replacing the cupola with a Bengali-style *chhatri* which was later removed by Governor General, Lord Hardinge in 1848, as it looked out of place, and now stands in the outer lawns of the complex, popularly known as Smith's Folly..

After an accident involving school children, entry to the Qutub Minar is closed to public since 1981, while Qutub archaeological area remains open for public,. In 2004, Seismic monitors were installed on the minar, which revealed in 2005 Delhi earthquake, no damage or substantial record of shakes. The reason for this has been cited as the use of lime mortar and rubble masonry which absorbs the tremors; it is also built on rocky soil, which further protects it during earthquakes.

Qubbat-ul-Islam Mosque

Qubbat-ul-Islam mosque (Might of Islam) (also known

as the *Qutb Mosque* or the *Great Mosque of Delhi*) was built by Qutb-ud-din Aybak, founder of the Mamluk or Slave dynasty. It was the first mosque built in Delhi after the Islamic conquest of India and the oldest surviving example of Ghurids architecture in Indian subcontinent. The construction of this Jami Masjid (Friday Mosque), started in the year 1193 AD, when Aibak was the commander of Muhammad Ghori's garrison that occupied Delhi. The Qutub Minar was built simultaneously with the mosque but appears to be a stand alone structure, built as the 'Minar of Jami Masjid', for the muezzin to perform adhan, call for prayer, and also as a *qutb*, an Axis or Pole of Islam. It is reminiscent in style and design of the *Arhai-din-ka Jhompra* or Ajmer mosque at Ajmer, Rajasthan, also built by Aibak during the same time, also constructed by demolishing earlier temples and a Sanskrit school, at the site.

According to a Persian inscription still on the inner eastern gateway, the mosque was built by the parts taken by destruction of twenty-seven Jain temples built previously during Tomars and Prithvi Raj Chauhan, and leaving certain parts of the temple outside the mosque proper. Historical records compiled by Muslim historian Maulana Hakim Saiyid Abdul Hai attest to the iconoclasm of Qutb-ud-din Aybak. This pattern of iconoclasm was common during his reign, although an argument goes that such iconoclasm was motivated more by politics than by religion.

The mosque is built on a raised and paved courtyard, measuring 141 ft. X 105 ft, surrounded by pillared cloisters added by Iltutmish between 1210 and 1220 AD. The stone screen between prayer hall and the courtyard, stood 16 mt at its highest was added in 1196 CE, the corbelled arches had Arabic inscriptions and motifs. Entrances to the courtyard, also uses ornate *mandap* dome from temples, whose pillars are used extensively throughout the edifice, and in the sanctuary beyond the tall arched screens. What survives today of the sanctuary on the western side are the arched screens in between, which once led to a series of aisles with low-domed ceilings for worshippers. Expansion of the mosque continued after the death of Qutb. Qutbuddin's successor Iltutmish, extended the original prayer hall screen by three more arches. By the time of Iltutmish, the Mamluk empire had stabilized enough that the Sultan could replace most of his conscripted Hindu masons with Muslims. This explains why the arches added under Iltutmish are stylistically more Islamic than the ones erected under Qutb's rule, also because the material used wasn't from demolished temples. Some additions to the mosque were also done by Alauddin Khilji, including the Alai Darwaza, the formal entrance to the mosque in red sandstone and white marble, and a court to the east of the mosque in 1300 AD.

The mosque is in ruins today but indigenous corbelled arches, floral motifs, and geometric patterns can be seen among the Islamic architectural structures. To the west of the Quwwat ul-Islam mosque is the tomb of Iltutmish which was built by the monarch in 1235.

Iron Pillar

The iron pillar is one of the world's foremost metallurgical curiosities. The pillar, 7.21 metre high and weighing more than six tonnes, was originally erected by Chandragupta II Vikramaditya (375–414 AD) in front of a Vishnu Temple complex at Udayagiri around 402 AD, and later shifted by Iltutmish from Udaygiri to its present location in the Qutub complex, sometime around 1233 AD.

The estimated weight of the decorative bell of the pillar is 646 kg while the main body weighs 5865 kg thereby making the entire pillar weigh at 6,511 kg. The pillar bears an inscription in Sanskrit in Brahmi script dating 4th century AD, which indicates that the pillar was set up as a *Vishnudhvaja*, standard of god Vishnu, on the hill known as Vishnupada in memory of a mighty king named Chandra, believed to Chandragupta II. A deep socket on the top of this ornate capital suggests that probably an image of Garuda was fixed into it, as common in such flagpoles.

Tomb of Iltutmish

The tomb of Slave Dynasty ruler, Iltutmish, the second Sultan of Delhi (r. 1211-1236 AD), built 1235 AD is also part of the Qutb complex at Mehrauli. The central chamber is a 9 mt sq. and has squinches, suggesting the existence of a dome, which has since collapsed. The main cenotaph, in white marble, is placed on a raised platform in the centre of the chamber. The facade is known for its ornate carving, both at the entrance and the interior walls. The interior west wall has a prayer niche (*mihrab*) decorated with marble, and a rich amalgamation of Hindu motives into Islamic architecture, such as bell-and-chain, tassel, lotus, diamond emblems.

Tomb of Imam Zamin

Tomb of Imam Muhammad Ali, or Imam Zamin, stand on a raised courtyard, next to the *Alai Darwaza*. According to an inscription of the eastern entrance to the tomb, Imam Zamin was a saint from Turkestan, who settled in India in around 1500, during the Sikander Lodhi. He built his tomb during his lifetime, and was buried here after his death in 1539 AD. The sandstone structure has dome on an octagonal base, while its interior is finished in polished white plaster, and contains fine, perforated *jalis*, or screens common in Lodhi period architecture.

Alauddin Khilji's Tomb and Madarsa

At the back of the complex, southwest of the mosque, stands an L-shaped construction, consisting of Alauddin Khilji's tomb dating ca 1316 CE, and a *madarsa*, an Islamic seminary built by him. Khilji was the second Sultan of Delhi from Khilji dynasty, who ruled from 1296 to 1316 AD.

The central room of the building, which has his tomb, has now lost its dome, though many rooms of the seminary or college are intact, and since been restored. It was the first example in India, of a tomb standing alongside a *madarsa*. Near by stands the Alai Minar, an ambitious tower, he started constructing to rival the Qutub Minar, though he died when only its first storey was built and its construction abandoned thereafter. It now stands, north of the mosque.

Alai Minar

Alauddin Khilji started building the Alai Minar, after he had doubled the size of Quwwat ul-Islam mosque. He conceived this tower to be two times higher than Qutb Minar in proportion with the enlarged mosque. The construction was however abandoned, just after the completion of the 24.5 meter high first storey core; soon after death of Ala-ud-din in 1316 AD, and never taken up by his successors of Khilji dynasty. The first story of the Alai Minar, a giant rubble masonry core, still stands today, which was evidently intended to be covered with dressed stone later on. Noted Sufi poet and saint of his times, Amir Khusro in his work, *Tarikh-i-Alai*, mentions Aladdin's intentions to extend the mosque and also constructing another minar.

Ala-ud-din conceived a very ambitious construction programme when he decided to build the second tower of victory when he returned in triumph from his Deccan campaign. However, the Sultan died before even the first storey was finished and the project was abandoned. Ala-ud-din, felt compelled to increase even further the size of the Quwwat-ul-Islam mosque. His scheme called for increasing the size of the enclosure four times, providing ceremonial entrance gateways on each side, and a great minar, twice the size of the Qutb. This is the unfinished base of the mammoth tower begun by Ala-ud-din Khilji intended to give competition to Qutb Minar.

Other Monuments

A short distance west of the enclosure, in Mehrauli village, is the Tomb of Adham Khan who, according to legend drove the beautiful Hindu singer Roopmati to suicide following the capture of Mandu in Madhya Pradesh. When Akbar became displeased with him he ended up being heaved off a terrace in the Agra Fort. Several archeological monuments dot the Mehrauli Archeological Park, including the Balban's tomb, Jamali Kamali mosque and tomb.

There are some summer palaces in the area, Zafar Mahal, Jahaz Mahal next to Hauz-i-Shamsi lake and the tombs of the later Mughal kings of Delhi, inside a royal enclosure near the dargah shrine of Sufi saint, Qutbuddin Bakhtiar Kaki. Here an empty space between two of the tombs, *sargah*, was intended for the last king of Delhi, who died in exile in Rangoon, Burma, in 1862, following his implication in the 1857 Indian Mutiny, also standing nearby is the *Moti Masjid* mosque in white marble.

Red Fort (Lal Qila)

The Red Fort, usually transcribed into English as Lal Qil'ah or Lal Qila is a 17th century fort complex constructed by the Mughal emperor Shahjahan in the walled city of Old Delhi. It served as the capital of the Mughals until 1857, when Mughal emperor Bahadur Shah Zafar was exiled by the British Indian government. The British used it as a military camp until India was made independent in 1947. It is now a popular tourist site, as well as a powerful symbol of India's sovereignty: the Prime Minister of India raises the flag of India on the rampants of the Lahori Gate of the fort complex every year on Independence Day. It was designated a UNESCO World Heritage Site in 2007.

In fact, Mughal Emperor Shahjahan, started construction of this massive fort in 1638 and work was completed in 1648 (10 years). The Red Fort was originally referred to as "Qila-i-Mubarak" (the blessed fort), because it was the residence of the royal family. The layout of the Red Fort was organised to retain and integrate this site with the Salimgarh Fort. The fortress palace was an important focal point of the medieval city of Shahjahanabad. The planning and aesthetics of the Red Fort represent the zenith of Mughal creativity which prevailed during the reign of Emperor Shah Jahan. This Fort has had many developments added on after its construction by Emperor Shahjahan. The significant phases of development were under Aurangzeb and later Mughal rulers. Important physical changes were carried out in the overall settings of the site after the First War of Independence during British Rule in 1857. After Independence, the site experienced a few changes in terms of addition/alteration to the structures. During the British period the Fort was mainly used as a cantonment and even after Independence, a significant part of the Fort remained under the control of the Indian Army until the year 2003.The Red Fort is a tourist attraction from around the world. The Red Fort was the palace for Mughal Emperor Shah Jahan's new capital, Shahjahanabad, the seventh city in the Delhi site. He moved his capital here from Agra in a move designed to bring prestige to his reign, and to provide ample opportunity to apply his ambitious building schemes and interests.

The fort lies along the Yamuna River, which fed the moats that surround most of the wall. The wall at its north-eastern corner is adjacent to an older fort, the Salimgarh Fort, a defense built by Islam Shah Suri in 1546.The construction of the Red Fort began in 1638 and was completed by 1648.

On 11 March 1783, Sikhs briefly entered Red Fort in Delhi and occupied the Diwan-i-Am. The city was essentially surrendered by the Mughal wazir in cahoots with his Sikh Allies. This task was carried out under the command of the Sardar Baghel Singh Dhaliwal of the Karor Singhia misl.

The last Mughal emperor to occupy the fort was Bahadur Shah II "Zafar". Despite being the seat of Mughal power and its defensive capabilities, the Red Fort was not defended during the 1857 uprising against the British. After the failure of the 1857 rebellion, Zafar left the fort on 17 September. He returned to Red Fort as a prisoner of the British. Zafar was tried on in a trial starting on 27 January 1858, and was exiled on 7 October.

Red Fort showcases the very high level of art form and ornamental work. The art work in the Fort is a synthesis of Persian, European and Indian art which resulted in the development of unique Shahjahani style which is very rich in form, expression and colour. Red Fort, Delhi is one of the important building complexes of India which encapsulates a long period of Indian history and its arts. Its significance has transcended time and space. It is relevant as a symbol of architectural brilliance and power. Even before its notification as a monument of national importance in the year 1913, efforts were made to preserve and conserve the Red Fort, for posterity.

The walls of the fort are smoothly dressed, articulated by heavy string-courses along the upper section. They open at two major gates, the Delhi and the Lahore gates. The Lahore Gate is the main entrance; it leads to a long covered bazaar street, the Chatta Chowk, whose walls are lined with stalls for shops. The Chatta Chowk leads to a large open space where it crosses the large north-south street that was originally the division between the fort's military functions, to its west, and the palaces, to its east. The southern end of this street is the Delhi Gate.

Main Structures inside the Fort

Diwan-i-Aam

Beyond this gate is another, larger open space, which originally served as the courtyard of the Diwan-i-Aam, the large pavilion for public imperial audiences with an ornate throne-balcony (*jharokha*) for the emperor. The columns were painted in gold and there was a gold and silver railing separating the throne from the public.

Diwan-i-Khas

The Diwan-i-Khas is a pavilion clad completely in marble, the pillars are decorated with floral carvings and inlay work with many semi-precious stones.

Nahr-i-Behisht

The imperial private apartments lie behind the throne. The apartments consist of a row of pavilions that sits on a raised platform along the eastern edge of the fort, looking out onto the river Yamuna. The pavilions are connected by a continuous water channel, known as the Nahr-i-Behisht, or the "Stream of Paradise", that runs through the centre of each pavilion. The water is drawn from the river Yamuna, from a tower, the *Shah Burj*, at the north-eastern corner of the fort. The palace is designed as an imitation of paradise as it is described in the Koran; a couplet repeatedly inscribed in the palace reads, "If there be a paradise on earth, it is here, it is here". The planning of the palace is based on Islamic prototypes, but each pavilion reveals in its architectural elements the Hindu influences typical of Mughal building. The palace complex of the Red Fort is counted among the best examples of the Mughal style.

Zenana

The two southernmost pavilions of the palace are *zenanas*, or women's quarters: the Mumtaz Mahal (now a museum), and the larger, lavish Rang Mahal, which has been famous for its gilded, decorated ceiling and marble pool, fed by the *Nahr-i-Behisht*.

Moti Masjid

To the west of the hammam is the Moti Masjid, the Pearl Mosque. This was a later addition, built in 1659 as a private mosque for Aurangzeb, Shah Jahan's successor. It is a small, three-domed mosque in carved white marble, with a three-arched screen which steps down to the courtyard.

Hayat Bakhsh Bagh

To its north lies a large formal garden, the Hayat Bakhsh Bagh, or "Life-Bestowing Garden", which is cut through by two bisecting channels of water. A pavilion stands at either end of the north-south channel, and a third, built in 1842 by the last emperor, Bahadur Shah Zafar, stands at the centre of the pool where the two channels meet.

The Red Fort is one of the most popular tourist destinations in Old Delhi, attracting thousands of visitors every year. The fort is also the site from which the Prime Minister of India addresses the nation on 15 August, the day India achieved independence from the British. It also happens to be the largest monument in Old Delhi.

At one point in time, more than 3,000 people lived within the premises of the Delhi Fort complex. But after the Sepoy Mutiny of 1857, the fort was captured by Britain and the residential palaces destroyed. It was made the headquarters of the British Indian Army. Immediately after the mutiny, Bahadur Shah Zafar was tried at the Red Fort. It was also here in November 1945, that the most famous courts-martial of three officers of the Indian National Army were held. After India gained independence in 1947, the Indian Army took control over the fort. In December 2003, the Indian Army handed the fort over to the Indian tourist authorities.

Today, a sound and light show describing Mughal history is a tourist attraction in the evenings. The general condition of the major architectural features is mixed. None of the water features, which are extensive, contain water. Some of the buildings are in fairly good condition and have their decorative elements undisturbed. In others, the marble inlay flowers have been removed by looters and vandals. The tea house, though not in its historical state, is a functioning restaurant. The mosque and hamam are closed to the public, though one can catch peeks through the glass windows or marble lattice work. Walkways are left mostly in a crumbling state. Public toilets are available at the entrance and inside the park, but some are quite unsanitary.

The entrance through the Lahore Gate leads to a retail mall with jewellery and crafts stores. There is a museum of "blood paintings" depicting young Indian martyrs of the 20th century along with the story of their martyrdom. There is also an archaeological museum and an Indian war memorial museum.

Fatehpuri Masjid

Fatehpuri Masjid is located at the western end of the oldest street of Delhi, Chandni Chowk. It thus counterbalances the Red Fort on the opposite end of Chandni Chowk. Fatehpuri Masjid was built in 1650 by Fatehpuri Begum, one of Shah Jahan's wives (*kaniz* i.e. concubine) who was from Fatehpur, and the mosque at Taj Mahal is also named after her.

The mosque is built using red sandstone and has a fluted dome with *mahapadma* and *kalash* on the top. Flanked by minarets, the mosque has a traditional design with the prayer hall having seven-arched openings. The mosque has single and double-storeyed apartments on the sides.

The central iwan in the middle is flanked by three arches on each side.

The British had auctioned the mosque after the 1857 war to Rai Lala Chunnamal for Rs. 19,000 (whose descendants still live in the Chunnamal haveli in Chandni Chowk), who preserved the mosque. Later in 1877 it was acquired by the government in exchange for four villages and was restored to the Muslims at the Delhi Durbar when the British allowed the Muslims back in Old Delhi. A similar mosque built by the Akbarabadi Begum was destroyed by the British.

- The Khari Baoli, which is today Asia's largest spice market, gradually developed after the construction of the mosque. Muslim festivals *Id-ul-Fitr* and *Id-ul-Zuha* are celebrated with great enthusiasm at the mosque.

Jama Masjid

Jama Masjid of Delhi, is the principal mosque of Old Delhi in India. Commissioned by the Mughal Emperor Shah Jahan, builder of the Taj Mahal, and completed in the year 1656 AD, it is the largest and best-known mosque in India. It lies at the origin of a very busy central street of Old Delhi, Chandni Chowk. The later name, Jama Masjid, is a reference to the weekly Friday noon congregation prayers of Muslims, Jummah, which are usually done at a mosque, the "congregational mosque" or "jâmi' masjid". The courtyard of the mosque can hold up to twenty-five thousand worshippers. The mosque also houses several relics in a closet in the north gate, including an antique copy of the Qur'an written on deer skin.

The foundation of the historic Jama Masjid (Friday Mosque) was laid on a hillock in Shahjahanabad by fifth Mughal Emperor of India, Shahjahan, on Friday the October 6, 1650 AD, (10th Shawwal 1060 AH). The mosque was the result of the efforts of over 5,000 workers, over a period of six years. The cost incurred on the construction in those times was 10 lakh (1 million) Rupees, and it was same

Emperor who also built the Taj Mahal, at Agra and the Red Fort, which stands across the Jama Masjid, which was finally ready in 1656 AD (1066 AH), complete with three great gates, four towers and two 40 m-high minarets constructed of strips of red sandstone and white marble.

It is pertinent to note that Shah Jahan built several important mosques in Delhi, Agra, Ajmer and Lahore. The Jama Masjid's floorplan is very similar to the Jama Masjid, Fatehpur Sikri near Agra, but the Jamia Masjid is the bigger and more imposing of the two. Its majesty is further enhanced because of the high ground that he selected for building this mosque. The architecture and design of the slightly larger Badshahi Mosque of Lahore built by Shah Jahan's son Aurangzeb in 1673 is closely related to the Jamia Masjid in Delhi.

The courtyard of the mosque can be reached from the east, north and south by three flights of steps, all built of red sandstone. The northern gate of the mosque has 39 steps. The southern side of the mosque has 33 steps. The eastern gate of the mosque was the royal entrance and it has 35 steps. These steps used to house food stalls, shops and street entertainers. In the evening, the eastern side of the mosque used to be converted into a bazaar for poultry and birds in general. Prior to the 1857 War of Indian Independence, there was a madrassah near the southern side of the mosque, which was pulled down after the mutiny. The mosque faces west. Its three sides are covered with open arched colonnades, each having a lofty tower-like gateway in the centre. The mosque is about 261 feet (80 m) long and 90 feet (27 m) wide, and its roof is covered with three domes with alternate stripes of black and white marble, with its topmost parts covered with gold. Two lofty minarets, 130 feet (41 m) high, and containing 130 steps, longitudinally striped with white marble and red sandstone, flank the domes on either side. The minarets are divided by three projecting galleries and are surmounted by open twelve-sided domed pavilions. On the back of the mosque, there are four small minarets crowned like those in the front.

Under the domes of the mosque, is a hall with seven arched entrances facing the west and the walls of the mosque, up to the height of the waist, are covered with marble. Beyond this is a prayer hall, which is about 61 meters X 27.5 meters, with eleven arched entrances, of which the centre arch is wide and lofty, and in the form of a massive gateway, with slim minarets in each corner, with the usual octagonal pavilion surmounting it. Over these arched entrances there are tablets of white marble, four feet (1.2 m) long and 2.5 feet (760 mm) wide, inlaid with inscriptions in black marble. These inscriptions give the history of the building of the mosque, and glorify the reign and virtues of Shah Jahan. The slab over the centre arch contains simply the words "The Guide!"

The mosque stands on a platform of about five feet (1.5 m) from the pavement of the terrace, and three flight of steps lead to the interior of the mosque from the east, north, and the south. The floor of the mosque is covered with white and black marble ornamented to imitate the Muslim prayer mat; a thin black marble border is marked for the worshippers, which is three feet long and 1 ½ feet wide. In total there are 899 such spaces marked in the floor of the mosque. The back of the mosque is cased over to the height of the rock on which the mosque stands with large hewn stones.

Salimgarh Fort

Salimgarh Fort was built in 1546 AD, in Delhi, in a former island of the Yamuna River, by Salim Shah Suri, son of Sher Shah Suri. There was a pause in Mughal rule when in 1540 AD Sher Shah Suri defeated the Mughal Emperor Humayun (and ousted him from Delhi) and established the Sur dynasty rule in Delhi. Sur dynasty rule lasted till 1555 AD when Humayun regained his kingdom by defeating Sikander Suri, the last ruler of the dynasty. During the Mughal period, in later years, while building the Red Fort and Shahjahanbad, several Mughal rulers including Emperor Shahjahan who is credited with completing Shahjahanabad in 1639 A.D. had camped at this fort. It is said that Humayun had camped at this fort for three days before launching his successful attack for recapturing Delhi.

Aurangzeb, the Mughal Emperor, converted the fort into a prison, which practice was perpetuated by the British who took control of the fort in 1857. The Fort is part of the Red Fort Complex. The complex was declared as a UNESCO World Heritage site in 2007, which obligates Archeological Survey of India (ASl) to ensure well planned conservation measures for the heritage monuments.

The location chosen for building the fortification was in the Delhi plains (with an elevation range of 80–110 feet (24–34 m), hemmed by the Yamuna River on one side and the northern spur of the Aravalli range of hills on the other side. This topography of the land area with the rock exposures at the Fort's location, with a favorable link with the northeast trending ridge and Juma Masjid, was visualized as an ideal setting that provided the needed protection against erosion by the Yamuna River. It was also obvious that a stream on one side and a mountain ridge on the other side of any fortification would be a formidable barrier for invaders to penetrate into Delhi, as such a setting would only force the invaders to follow the river course.

Keeping these advantages in view the Salimgarh Fort was built in 1546. However, Humayun after he won back the Empire had renamed Salimghar Fort as "Nurghar" since the first ruler of Sur Dynasty, Sher Shah Suri (father of Salim Shah Suri who had built the fort) had earlier usurped his Kingdom in 1540 AD. He had, therefore, decreed that nobody would use its original name in his court. During the British rule, the Sepoy Mutiny (also called the First War of Independence (the Upraising) was put down in 1857 and the last Mughal Emperor Bahadur Shah Zafar II was taken prisoner at Humayun tomb. This fort was then the scene of lot of war activity. During the Upraising, Emperor Bahadur Shah II's complicity with the mutinous soldiers was obvious. He operated from this Fort.

During August and early September 1857 he held meetings at the fort on war strategy. He also watched, from the ramparts of the fort, artillery fire aimed at the British Army. He even played a psychological game with his army officers who had come in a delegation seeking salary, when he told them that he would forego some of his crown jewels for the purpose and that he would give up his life for the cause; the officers refused his offer trusting that the Emperor was stating all this in right earnest. Following this, even proclamations were issued declaring that the Emperor would lead the attack against the British and urging all his people, irrespective of caste or creed, to join him in fighting the war. But, in the middle of September 1857, British soldiers were closing in on the Fort.

At this stage, his trusted assistant Bhakt Khan urged the Emperor to leave the fort and accompany him to a safer place and look for a day when he could "renew war in the open country". But the Emperor refused, permitted his army to vacate the fort but he himself moved to the Humayun tomb. The fourth infantry of the British army entered the Salimgarh Fort where they encountered a single sentry only. Similar experience was encountered by the Punjab Fourth infantry regiment when, earlier, they had entered the Palace from the Lahore gate of the Red Fort. After the Uprising was put down, the fort was, for a time, used by the British as an army camp (with artillery units) but was subsequently, from 1945, used as a penitentiary to incarcerate the Indian Freedom Fighters of the Indian National Army (INA).

The Fort has a triangular plan and its thick walls are built in rubble masonry. It has circular bastions. From the time it was built, the fort structure has undergone several stages of repairs over the centuries. An Arch bridge links it with Red Fort on the northeastern side, which was constructed during Bahadur Shah Zafar's reign and hence the gate is named as Bahadur Shah Gate. The gate is built of brick masonry with selective use of red sandstone. During the British rule, a railway line was constructed, after demolishing an old bridge, which divided the Salimgarh Fort and chipped part of the Red Fort, and which was then considered an uncaring action. This railway line has truncated the fort.

As a Prison

Unfortunately, during Aurangzeb's reign, the fort was first converted into a prison. Aurangzeb had imprisoned his brother Murad Baksh (whom he had caught unawares while sleeping after a drinking binge at Mutra) who had acted as his confidant and supporter during his fight with his elder brother Dara Shikoh, at this fort for reasons of "apostasy for abandoning the fundamental tenets of Islam". He was later shifted to Gwalior where he was executed. It is also said that Auranagzeb, apart from imprisoning Murad Baksh, had the dubious credit of incarcerating his favourite eldest daughter Zebunnisa in the Salimgarh Fort for 21 years till her death.

It was stated that she was imprisoned for being a poetess and a musician (both anathema to Aurangzeb's austere, more orthodox and fundamental way of life and thinking) and for being sympathetic to her brother Muhammad Akbar who was persona non–grata with the Emperor. The British had kept Bahadur Shah incarcerated at this the fort, after he was taken prisoner at Humayun tomb and later shifted to Rangoon, Burma.

The Fort has been compared to the Tower of London in England where state prisoners were either tormented to death or faded away in the prison. Before India got Independence from the British Rule, freedom fighters of Indian National Army (INA) were also imprisoned and tortured in this fort from 1945 till India's independence in August 1947. Hence, Salimghar Fort is now renamed as Swatantrata Senani Smarak in memory of the freedom fighters who died in this fort prison.

Ghosts are said to haunt the fort area and several stories are narrated in this regard. One of them relates to Zebunnisa wearing a black veil singing poems composed by her, on moonlit nights. It is also mentioned that the moans and groans of the soldiers of INA who were tortured and who died here are heard in the vicinity. Thus, this fort established a strong link between the Mughal rule and the British rule.

The fort which had been continuously occupied by the Army, from the time of first independence movement in 1857 till 2005, was initially under the British army control with artillery units headquartered there and also as a prison, and subsequently it was under the control of the Indian Army after India's Independence on August 15, 1947. Several other government agencies, including ASI, were also involved with the upkeep of the monuments. This became an issue when ASI had approached UNESCO in 1992 to include this monument for inscription on World Heritage List. Hence, at that time ASI withdrew the application for listing by UNESCO.

The multi control of the Fort was causing problems to the ASI in taking adequate conservation measures to protect and preserve this monument, along with the Red Fort and other monuments within the fort complex. ASI had petitioned the Courts through an affidavit stating: "It is impossible to maintain these portions of the Fort unless and until they are completely vacated and handed over to the ASI for proper assessment of the damage already caused". ASI had also stated that the Ministry of Tourism of the Government of India would approach the UNESCO to accord world heritage status to the monument once it was transferred to their complete jurisdiction and after completing the needed restoration works. The Army transferred the fort to ASI's possession in December, 2003 and thereafter, in 2006, the ASI submitted its proposal for World Heritage listing by UNESCO. Finally, the World Heritage Committee accepted Government of India's request and accorded approval for inscription of the Red Fort Complex, Delhi in the World Heritage List, in its meeting held from 23 to 27 June, 2007 at Christchurch, New Zealand. The Press release issued by the ASI, after UNESCO listing was approved, states:

> The core zone of about hectare includes the Red Fort and Salimgarh Fort while the buffer zone measuring over 40 hectares includes the immediate surroundings of the Red Fort and Salimgarh Fort. The Red Fort Complex, Delhi is classified as a cultural property with an outstanding universal significance. The inscription of the Red Fort on the World Heritage List is very significant for Delhi since the Red Fort Complex would be the third World Heritage Site in the city, an honour that no other single location in the country can boast of.

Further to the above listing, ASI at the directive of the Supreme Court of India, prepared a draft report presenting a "Comprehensive Conservation Management Plan (CCMP)" based on a detailed study of the site's importance. The plan has taken due cognizance of the role and duties of management of the fort by various departments and agencies that operated from within the Fort. The plan also envisages restoration of the old bridge that links Red Fort to Salimgarh since it provides historical link between the Mughal Rule and the British Rule.

Till the time the CCMP is approved and items of work are prioritized, ASI has undertaken several restoration actions in the Red Fort at a cost of Rs 275 lakhs (US $0.55 million) and at Salimgarh Fort at a cost of Rs 80 lakhs (US$160,000) to be completed before the 2010 Commonwealth Games.

Museum

The Swatantra Sangram Museum, which opened to the public on October 2, 1995, is located in the precincts of the Red Fort Complex within the Salimgarh Fort as it was the prison where the INA Freedom fighters were incarcerated by the British from 1945 till Independence of India from

British rule on 15 August 1947. Many of the freedom fighters had died within the jail premises. The place was chosen as the site for the Museum on the basis of initial identification provided by a geriatric Colonel Gurbaksh Singh Dhillon (one of the heroes of the Indian National Army) of the location where the British had held trial of the Indian National Army freedom fighters for treason, in 1945. Since then he retracted (after the present museum was completed) his selection of the site and indicated a new building adjoining the existing museum as the site where the trial was held. In 2007 (the 60th Year of India's Independence), ASI decided to shift the Museum to the new location but with more documents for the new galleries, apart from providing better lighting, paneling, and displays for existing structures.

On this occasion, a section on Mahatma Gandhi was also proposed to be added to the Museum with full–size depictions of the Jallianwala Bagh firing and the Salt Satyagraha. At the Prime Minister's intervention the premises of the fort and the Museum have been opened to the public. To encourage tourists to visit this place, ASI has also introduced guides at the Red Fort gate to give directions to this Fort, which till recently was hardly known to the public vis-à-vis the famous Red Fort. Also, the long walk from the Red Fort gate to this place discouraged people from visiting the fort and the museum.

How to Reach?

In the initial years, the Fort was accessed through boats only but a bridge linking the Red Fort with Salimgarh Fort was said to have been built by Jahangir, father of Shahajahan;a conflicting information also attributes its construction by Farid Khan who held the fort in Jagir. This bridge was later replaced by a railway bridge at the same location. At present, an arched over bridge connects it from the Red Fort end. From this location, the fort provides a commanding view of the Red Fort, the river and the surroundings.

But it is a noisy area with continuous flow of heavy traffic from the several artery roads that surround it and also from the traffic flow from the trans–Yamuna over the existing steel bridge on the main river close by. The East India Railway was brought to Delhi through the Salimgarh Fort. The line used to pass over Salimgarh and a portion of the fort. It was later extended to the Rajputana Railway.

Hauz Khas Complex

Hauz Khas Complex in South Delhi houses a water tank, an Islamic seminary, a mosque, a tomb and pavilions built around an urbanized village with medieval history traced to the thirteenth century of Delhi Sultanate reign. It was part of Siri, the second medieval city of India of the Delhi Sultanate of Allauddin Khilji Dynasty (1296–1316). The etymology of the name Hauz Khas in Urdu language is derived from the words 'Hauz': "water tank" (or lake) and 'Khas':"royal"- the "Royal tank". The large water tank or reservoir was first built by Khilji {the plaque displayed (pictured in the gallery) at the site records this fact} to supply water to the inhabitants of Siri. The tank was de–silted during the reign of Firuz Shah Tughlaq (1351–88). Several buildings (Mosque and madrasa) and tombs were built overlooking the water tank or lake. Firuz Shah's tomb pivots the L–shaped building complex which overlooks the tank.

Remarkably, the 1980s, the Hauz Khas village, studded with domed tombs of Muslim royalty from the fourteenth century to sixteenth century, was developed as an upper class residential cum commercial area in the metropolis of South Delhi, India. It is now a major expensive tourist cum commercial area with numerous art galleries, posh restaurants and upscale boutiques.

The water tank that was excavated during Alauddin Khilji's reign (1296–1316) in the second city of Delhi to meet the water supply needs of the newly built fort at Siri, was originally known as Hauz-i-Alai after Khilji. But Firuz Shah Tughlaq (1351–88) of the Tughlaq dynasty re-excavated the silted tank and cleared the clogged inlet channels. The tank was originally of about 50 ha (123.6 acres) area with dimensions of 600 m (1,968.5 ft) width and 700 m (2,296.6 ft) length with 4 m (13.1 ft) depth of water. When built, its storage capacity at the end of each monsoon season was reported to be 0.8 Mcum. Now the tank size has substantially reduced due to encroachment and siltation but is well maintained in its present state. Feruz Shah who ruled from his new city called the Firuzabad (now known as Feroz Shah Kotla) – the fifth city of Delhi – was an enlightened ruler. He was known for "his keen sense of historical precedent, statements of dynastic legitimacy and the power of monumental architecture". He is credited with construction of new monuments (several mosques and palaces) in innovative architectural styles, irrigation works and renovating/restoring old monuments such as the Qutub Minar, Sultan Ghari and Suraj Kund, and also erecting two inscribed Ashokan Pillars, which he had transported from Ambala and Meerut in Delhi. At Hauz Khas, he raised several monuments on the southern and eastern banks of the reservoir.

In efforts made in the past by the Delhi Development Authority to develop Hauz Khas village, the inlets to the reservoir were blocked and consequently the lake had gone dry for several years. To rectify the situation, a plan was implemented in 2004 to store storm water generated at the southern ridge of Delhi behind an embankment and then diverting it into the lake. An outside source has also been tapped by feeding the water from the treatment plant at Sanjay Van into the lake. With these efforts initiated by The Indian National Trust for Art and Cultural Heritage (INTACH), the lake has been revived.

The notable structures built by Firuz Shah on the eastern and northern side of the reservoir consisted of the Madrasa (Islamic School of Learning – a theological college), the small, Mosque, the Main tomb for himself and six domed pavilions in its precincts, which were all built between 1352 and 1354 A.D.

Madrasa

Established in 1352, the Madrasa was one of the leading institutions of Islamic learning in the Delhi Sultanate. It was also considered the largest and best equipped Islamic seminary anywhere in the world. There were three main Madrasa's in Delhi during Firuz Shah's time. One of them was the Firuz Shahi madrasa at Hauz Khas. After the sack of Baghdad, Delhi became the most important place in the world for Islamic education. The village surrounding the Madarsa was also called Tarababad (city of joy) in view of its affluent and culturally rich status, which provided the needed supporting sustenance supply system to the Madrasa.

The madrasa structure has an innovative design. It was built in L-Shape as one contiguous structure on the south and east edges of the reservoir complex. One arm of the L-shape structure runs in the North–South direction measuring 76 m (249.3 ft) and the other arm runs in the

East–West direction measuring 138 m (452.8 ft). The two arms are pivoted at the large Tomb of Firuz Shah (pictured). At the northern end there is a small mosque. Between the mosque and the tomb two storied pavilions exist now on the northern side and similar pavilions on the eastern side, overlooking the lake, which were used as madrasa. The two arms are interconnected through small domed gateways passing through the tomb at the center. The North–South arm with balconies overlooking the reservoir is a two storied building with three towers of varying sizes. Ornamental brackets cover the upper storied balconies while the lower stories have corbelled support. Roof overhangs or Eaves(chajjas) are seen now only in the upper stories though it is said that they existed on both stories when it was built.

From each floor of the Madrasa, staircases are provided to go down to the lake. Many cenotaphs, in the form of octagonal and square chhatris are also seen, which are reported to be possibly tombs of teachers of the Madrasa.

It is inferred that, though no regular curriculum could be cited, subjects taught in the Madrasa could have been *tafsix* (astronomy), *hadith* (mathematics), *qirat* (medicine), *ishlaq* (calligraphy), *kalàm* (grammar) and *fiqr* (oratory). Later on, Sanskrit was also taught. It is recorded that the first Director of the Madarasa was

> *one Jalal al-Din Rumi who knew fourteen sciences, could recite the Quran according to the seven known methods of recitation and had complete mastery over the five standard collections of the Traditions of the Prophet*

The madrasa was well tended with liberal donations from the Royalty. Timur, the Mongol ruler, who invaded Delhi, defeated Mohammed Shah Tughlaq in 1398 and plundered Delhi, had camped at this venue. Expressed in his own words, his impressions of the tank and buildings around Hauz Khas were vividly described as:

> When I reached [the city's] gates, I carefully reconnoitered its towers and walls, and then returned to the side of the Hauz Khas. This is a reservoir, which was constructed by Sultan Feruz Shah, and is faced all round with stone and stucco. Each side of the reservoir is more than a bows–shot long, and there are buildings placed around it. This tank is filled by rains in the rainy season, and it supports the people of the city with water throughout the year. The tomb of Sultan Firuz Shah stands on its bank

While his description of the place is correct but his ascribing construction of the tank to Firuz Shah was a misconception.

Pavilions

The madrasa is flanked by the reservoir in the northern front and by a garden on its southern side at the second floor level. The entry to the garden is from the eastern gate which paases through the Hauz Khas village. The garden houses six impressive pavilions. The pavilions with domes are in different shapes and sizes (rectangular, octagonal and hexagonal) and on the basis of inscriptions are inferred to be graves. A cluster of three hemispherical domes, a large one of 5.5 m (18.0 ft) diameter and two smaller ones of 4.5 m (14.8 ft) diameter, portray exquisite architectural features of foliated motifs on the drums with kalasa motifs on top of the domes. Each pavilion is raised on a plinth of about 0.8 m (2.6 ft) and is supported by square shaped wide columns with entablature which have decorative capitals that support beams with projecting canopies. Ruins of a courtyard with a rectangular plan, are seen to the west of the three pavilions which are built of double columns. The pavilions and the court yard are conjectured to have been used as part of the madrasa in the past. Another striking structure in the garden, opposite to the Feruz Shah's tomb on the southern side, is a small eight pillared Chatri seen in the garden which has large cantilevered beams that supported flat eaves all round the small dome.

Mosque

The northern end of the madrasa is secured to a small mosque. The qibla of the Mosque projects towards the reservoir by about 9.5 m (31.2 ft). A domed gateway from the south east provides entry into three rooms of size5.3 m (17.4 ft) x2.4 m (7.9 ft) whose utility is not traced. A "C"-shaped layout of a double row of pillars on a raised podium forms the prayer hall, which is open to the sky. The qibla wall seen clearly from the reservoir side has five mihrabs. The avant–garde setting of the central mihrab with a domed chhatri (cupola) with open sides is seen in the form of a pavilion projecting into the reservoir. The other mihrabs are set, on either side of the main mihrab, in the walls with grilled windows.

Firuz Shah Tomb

Firuz Shah, who established the tomb, ascended the throne in 1351 (inherited from his cousin Muhammad) when he was middle aged, as the third ruler of the Khilji dynasty and ruled till 1388. He was considered a well–liked ruler. His wife was a Hindu lady and his trusted Prime Minister, Khan-i-Jahan Junana Shah was a Hindu convert. Firuz Shah assisted by his Prime Minister was responsible for building several unique monuments (mosques, tombs, pavilions), hunting lodges and irrigation projects (reservoirs) in his domains, apart from establishing and constructing a new Citadel (palace) in his new city of Firuzabad. Feruz died at the age of ninety due to infirmities caused by three years of illness between 1385 and 1388. On his death, his grandson Ghiya Suddin was proclaimed as his successor to the throne. During his enlightened rule he abolished many vexatious taxes, brought in changes in the laws on capital punishment, introduced regulations in administration and discouraged lavish living styles.

But the most important credit that is bestowed on him is for the large number of public works executed during his reign namely, 50 dams for irrigation across rivers, 40 mosques, 30 colleges, 100 carvansarais, 100 hospitals, 100 public baths, 150 bridges, apart from many other monuments of aesthetic beauty and entertainment. Among the notable buildings of historical importance that he built within Hauz Khas precincts is the domed tomb for himself. The tomb which is very austere in appearance, is located at the intersection of the two arms of the L–shaped building which constitutes the madrasa. Entry to the tomb is through a passage in the south leading to the doorway. The passage wall is raised on a plinth which depicts the shape of a fourteen phased polyhedron built in stones. Three horizontal units laid over eight vertical posts that are chamfered constitute the plinth. Squinches and muqarnas are seen in the solid interior walls of the tomb and these provide the basic support to the octagonal sherical dome of the tomb.

The dome with a square plan – 14.8 m (48.6 ft) in length and height – has a diameter of 8.8 m (28.9 ft). The maximum height of the tomb is on its face overlooking the reservoir. The domed gateway on the north has an opening which has height equal to two–thirds the height of the tomb. The width of the gate is equal to one-third of tombs' width. The entrance hall has fifteen bays and terminates in another doorway which is identical to the gateway at the entrance. This second doorway leads to the tomb chamber and cenotaph, which are accessed from the gateway through the L–shaped corridor. Similar arrangement is replicated on the western doorway of the tomb leading to the open pavilion on the west. The ceiling in the dome depicts a circular gold medallion with Quranic inscriptions in Naksh characters. Foliated crenellations are seen on the outer faces of the base of the tomb. Interesting features seen on the northern and southern sides of the tomb, considered typical of the Tuglaq period layout, are the ceremonial steps provided at the ground level that connect to the larger steps leading into the reservoir.

The tomb, a square chamber, is made of local quartzite rubble with a surface plaster finish that sparkled in white colour when completed. The door, pillars and lintels were made of grey quartzites while red sandstone was used for carvings of the battlements. The door way depicts a blend of Indian and Islamic architecture. Another new feature not seen at any other monument in Delhi, built at the entrance to the tomb from the south, is the stone railings. There are four graves inside the tomb, one is of Feruz Shah and two others are of his son and grandson. The tomb was repaired during the reign of Sikandar Lodhi in 1507 AD, as is evidenced from an inscription on the entrance. The main impression is one of solidity and lack of decoration(typical of Tuglaq style).

The Village

The Hauz Khas village which was known in the medieval period for the amazing buildings built around the reservoir drew a large congregation of Islamic scholors and students to the Madrasa for Islamic education. A very well researched essay titled "A Medieval Center of Learning in India: The Hauz Khas Madrasa in Delhi" authored by Anthony Welch of the University of Victoria, Victoria, British Columbia, refers to this site as "far and away the finest spot in Delhi not in the ingenuity of its construction and the academic purpose to which it was put but also in the real magic of the place".

The present status of the village also retains not only the old charm of the place but has enhanced its aesthetic appeal through the well manicured green parks planted with ornamental trees all around with walk ways, and the sophisticated "gentrified" market and residential complexes which have sprung up around the old village. The tank itself has been reduced in size and well landscaped with water fountains. Welch, elaborating on the present status of the place, has said:"A centre of Musical culture in the fourteenth century, the village at the Hauz Khas had regained this erstwhile role in an unexpected guise."

The village structure that gloriously existed in the medieval period was modernized in mid 1980's presenting an upscale ambience attracting tourists from all parts of the world. The village complex is surrounded by Safdarjung Enclave, Green Park, South Extension, Greater Kailash. There are some of the India's most prestigious institutes situated in the neighbourhood including Indian Institute of Technology, Delhi, Indian Institute of Foreign Trade, National Institute of Fashion Technology, and All India Institute of Medical Sciences.

Lal Masjid

The Lal Masjid of Delhi, also known as the Fakrul Masjid, is a mosque located in Bara Bazaar, Kashmiri Gate. It was built in 1728-29 by Kaniz-i-Fatima (entitled

Fakr-i-Jahan), in memory of her husband Shujaat Khan, a noble in Aurangzeb's court. The mosque was included in Colonel James Skinner's estate, and is sometimes wrongly attributed to him.

Sultan Ghari

Sultan Ghari was the first Islamic Mausoleum (tomb) built in 1231 AD for Prince Nasiru'd-Din Mahmud, eldest son of Iltumish, in the "funerary landscape of Delhi" in the Malakapur village (near Vasant Kunj). Iltumish was the first Sultan of the Slave Dynasty who ruled in Delhi from 1210 to 1236 A.D. The area where the Ghari (meaning: cave) tomb is situated, was part of the first city of medieval Delhi known as the Slave Dynasty that ruled during the period 1206 to 1290.This area is now part of the Qutb complex. The Slave Dynasty was the forerunner under the early Delhi Sultanate that ruled from 1216 to 1516. This dynastic city was followed by creation of other five cities of Delhi ruled by different dynastic rulers of the Delhi Sultanate, namely, the Khilji dynasty (1290-1320), the Tughlaq dynasty (1320-1413), the Sayyid dynasty (1414-51), and the Lodi dynasty (1451-1526). The rule of the Mughal Empire then followed and lasted from 1526 to 1857.

The crypt or the tomb is implanted in a Ghari (cave), approached by winding steep stairs made of stone, and supported by pillars and flooring. The cave is covered by an unusual octagonal roof slab. The exterior of the tomb structure built in Delhi sandstone with marble adornment exhibits a walled area with bastions (towers) on corners, which impart it the look of a fortress in aesthetic Persian and Oriental architecture. The other tombs inside the Ghari have not been identified.

Iltumish, ruling from Delhi since 1210 A.D., invaded eastern India in 1225 A.D. to capture Laknauti (now a ruined city in West Bengal called Gaur). The resultant battle ended in signing of a Treaty between Izaz, the then ruler of Eastern India (Bihar and Bengal) and Iltumish; the former ruler agreeing to pay a surety of 80 lakh tankas (silver currency), 38 elephants, mint and issue of coins in the name of Iltumish and accepting Sultan's suzerainty over the region. Before returning to Delhi, Iltumish divided the region into Bihar and Lakhnauti, and installed Alauddin masud jani as his feudatory in Lakhnauti. But Jani's control was short lived as he was overthrown by Iwaz soon after Iltumish's departure.

There after, Iltutmish deputed his eldest son prince Nasiru'd-Din Mahmud to fight Iwaz. In the battle which took place near Lakhnauti, Iwaz was trounced and executed in 1227 A.D., along with his nobles. Prince Nasiru'd-Din Mahmud who was then appointed as governor of Lakhnauti province, merged his original province of Oudh with Bengal and Bihar, and established his capital at Lakhnauti. This act of his coupled with the fact that he was son of Iltumish enhanced his prestige in the province.

As a reward, he was given the honorific title of 'Malik-us-Sharq' (king of the East) by Iltutmish. His rule was short lived, eventful and he could consolidate his territory. But after a short rule of 18 months, Nasiru'd-Din Mahmud was killed. Immensely grieved by the death of his favourite eldest son, Iltumish built a tomb called the Sultan Ghari in memory of his son, in 1231 A.D., close to the Qutb complex.

Five years later, Iltumish died in the year 1236 and his tomb can be seen in the Qutb complex. His two other sons, namely Ruknuddin Feroze Shah (died 1237 A.D., after he was deposed) and Muizzudin Bahram Shah (was killed in 1241 A.D.) who ruled for short periods, before and after their famous sister Razia Sultan ruled Delhi, were also buried in separate Chhatris (cenotaphs), just next to the Sultan Ghari. One of the two Chhatris (pictured) is restored while the other has been destroyed. Some archelogical findings reported by the Archeological Survey of India are a) the inscription of 1361 recording the excavation of a tank on the occasion of a marriage, b) a stone linga (phallic symbol of Lord Shiva the Hindu God in a lintel) and c) a dilapitated mosque of Sultan Feroz Shah Tughlaq's time and a few scattered remnanats of the Mughal period.

The plan of the tomb structure is unusual. It is in the form of a fortress with a courtyard like layout, not common among tombs. It is built over a raised plinth of certain height in rubble masonry work. The octagonal shape of the tomb is also unique as it has been built within the fortress like outer structure with four corner towers, over a Ghari (cave) in front of the western Qibla wall of the mosque. It, thus, is a combination of an over ground tomb with towers (which is common in most of the tombs) and an underground chamber for the crypt.

The octagonal grave–chamber with the crypt (tomb) in an underground opening is supported on four columns raised with two pillars each that support beams, and depict ancient Indian temple relics both on the columns and on the floor. The roof of the chamber is built in thick lime–concrete. The western qibla (prayer wall) which has the mihrab, is made of marble in exquisite Turkish and Afghan design. The marble mihrab also has inscriptions from the Quran. The front elevation of this west wall has a marble facade, dated to Feroze Shah's rule (1351-88). The prayer chamber in front of the qibla depicts a *yoni-patta* (the base slab of a Linga.

The entire tomb depicts a trabeate or corbel arch construction, which was common in India before the true arch design of the Romans was introduced, which are seen in subsequent Islamic monuments. Feroz Shah Tughlaq (1351–1388 A.D.) is credited to have repaired the tomb, which had been substantially damaged. The Chhatri, a stand alone structure, next to the Sultan Garhi, a tomb of one of the two sons of Iltumish, was also restored during Firuz Shah's reign. Old village ruins surround the tomb. Old ruins of a Tugluq mosque, Jami masjid and a khanqah (a place of spiritual retreat) are also located on the southern side of the tomb.

The tomb is a revered place for devotees of both Hindu and Muslim religious communities of the nearby villages of Mahipalpur and Rangpur since they consider the tomb as the dargah of a saintly 'peer'; a visit to the tomb is more or less mandatory for newlyweds from these two villages. Because of the religious veneration, the monument is maintained better by the local people than the Archeological Survey of India who are the formal custodians to maintain the heritage structure.

Thursday is a special day for worship at this tomb when devotees, both Hindus and Muslims, visit the shrine, which represents a festive display of Hindu – Muslim syncretism of religious tolerance. Every year, on the 17th day of the Islamic month of Ziqad (month occurring between Ramadan and Eid festivals), the "Urs (death anniversary) of Nasiruddin Shah" is held when pilgrims from all parts of Delhi visit the tomb.

The heritage area of Sultan Ghari extends to 25 ha

(61.8 acres), which has been zoned as per the topographical features to implement appropriate restoration and conservation actions. In order to restore this monument, which has been declared as a Grade A Monument by the Indian National Trust for Art and Cultural Heritage (INTACH), the Delhi Urban Heritage Foundation evolved a Plan combining restoration works along with creation of a pleasant environmental ambience to bring out its ancient glory. This plan is under implementation by the Delhi Development Authority.

The Delhi Development Authority has undertaken the following construction activities :

1. The entrance gates of the Tomb (pictured) have been built with dolphur sandstones to match with the architectural setting of the Sultan Ghari tomb, adopting the same technique as used for building the domes
2. 100 m of restricted area and 200 m of regulated area are demarcated and fenced and four approach paths/ tracks constructed that lead to the main tomb
3. A water conservation plan (water harvesting) has also been evolved to partially meet the water requirements for the park around the tomb
4. ASI's control extends only up to 300 m from the tomb since the rest of the area surrounding it is proposed for urban development by the Army.

Sultan Ghari is located near Malakpur Kohli village on the Mehrauli–Palam Road, 8 km west of Qutb complex from Andheria More in present day South Delhi. The C–Block of Vasant Kunj, a modern suburb of Delhi, is just across the tomb.

Moth Ki Masjid

Moth Ki Masjid is a mosque located in Delhi, and was built in 1505 by Wazir Miya Bhoiya, Prime Minister during the reign of Sultan Sikander Lodi (1517–26). It was a new type of mosque developed by the Lodi dynasty in the fourth city of the medieval Delhi of the Delhi Sultanate. The name of the mosque literally translated into English language means 'Lentil Mosque' and this name tag 'Lentil' has an interesting legend. This mosque was considered a beautiful Dome (Gumbad) structure of the period.

The mosque is now completely enclosed within the modern locality of South Extension Part II, Uday Park and Masjid Moth comprising residential and commercial establishments in the urban setting of South Delhi.

It is famously narrated that when Sultan Sikandar Lodi was on a visit to a mosque in the vicinity of the present location of the Moth Ki Masjid for prayer, he knelt over a grain of moth (a kind of lentil), which had been dropped by a bird. His loyal Prime Minister Wazir Miya Bhoiya, who had accompanied the King, saw the lentil seed and observed that: A seed so honoured by His majesty must not be thrown away. It must be used in the service of God.

So he took the moth seed and planted it in his garden for further growth. Over the years, the process of repeated planting and replanting of the moth seeds was carried out. In this process, the seeds multiplied several times. The Wazir finally sold the rich harvest and earned good money. With the proceeds of the sale he built the mosque after seeking permission from the Sultan to construct the Mosque. Impressed by the ingenuity of his minister, Sikandar Lodi laid the foundation for building the mosque. Another version of the legend is that Sikandar Lodhi on one of his visits to the area played a prank on his Prime Minister by giving him a gift of a grain of moth (lentil). The Wazir accepted the gift in good grace and instead of throwing it away planted it in his garden. Over the years repeated plantation resulted in a rich harvest that provided a surplus income to the Wazir. Thereafter, the wazir, with the revenue earned from the lentil grains, decided to build a mosque. On completion, he invited the Sultan to visit the mosque and narrated the sequence of events which lead to the building of the mosque. Impressed by this unique achievement, the Lodi named the mosque as "Moth Ki Masjid" or the Mosque from the Moth Lentil.

Raised on a high plinth, the mosque has a square layout. It is approached from the eastern side street of village Moti Masjid, through an exquisitely designed gate made of red, blue, black and white coloured sandstones arranged in a neat design (see picture). In particular, the arch of the gateway has a Hindu arch within a Muslim arch. Up the gateway steps, the entry is into a large courtyard of 38.6 m (126.6 ft) width surrounded by walls. Within the courtyard, on the western side is the main shrine or the mosque with the rectangular prayer hall porch, which has a façade of five arched openings. The corners of the rectangular prayer hall are adorned with double storied towers. The towers have arched openings at the rear end of the roof with domed octagonal chhatris (the Cenotophs) on the related walls. The west side wall is provided with tapering turrets that depict a sophisticated outline (pictured).

The Cenotophs were the first of its kind to be built in India and since then these have been replicated in several other monuments, even in the Deccan. There are three impressive domes inside the prayer hall with the Mihrab located on the west qibla wall of the central dome, which is the largest of the three domes. The Mihrab depicts Quranic inscriptions in flora Nakashi in Iranian design. Turrets project out of the qibla. The central dome is supported on squinches. The domes on both flanks are borne on muqarnas pendentives. Carved panels of red sandstone and white marble and plaster, as well as glazed tiles embellish the walls of the mosque.

The overall effect of the Mosque has been best described as:

> epitomizes in itself all that is best in Architecture of the Lodis and displays a freedom of imagination, a bold diversity of design, an appreciation of contrasting light and shade and a sense of harmony in line and colour, which combine to make it one of the most spirited and picturesque buildings of its kind in the whole range of Islamic art.

It is also said that it was the private mosque of the builder.

An unusual feature of this mosque built in Indo–Islamic style of architecture is that it has an austere design with no minarets, calligraphic decorations and embellishments, which are otherwise traditional features of mosques. The dome is semicircular and windows have latticework screens. An architectural appreciation of the structure vis-à-vis the five arched façade of domes of the period aptly infers:

> the rapid crystallization of the earlier concept. Firstly, it is considerably larger than its predecessor. Secondly, the articulation of the recessed arches is far more adept. Thirdly, embellishment has been done using elegant niches on the columns abutting the arches. Another

important feature is the use of better material and color, as if the masons were trying for something more permanent and forceful.

The monument is located in South Delhi and is well connected by road. Delhi International Airport is 21 km (13.0 mi) away. There are no visitor charges and is open on all days from sunrise to sun set. There are several tourist attractions in the neighborhood of the Mosque, such as the Hauz Khas, Siri Fort, Kalkaji Temple, Lotus Temple, Nizamuddin Auliya and Chirag Dehlvi's Dargah.

Siri Fort

Siri Fort, in the city of New Delhi, was built during the rule of Ala-ud-Din Khalji of the Delhi Sultanate to defend the city from the onslaught of the Mongols. It was the second of the seven cities of medieval Delhi built around 1303 (stated to be the first entirely constructed by Muslims), which at present is seen only in ruins with a few remnants.

Near the Siri Fort ruins modern auditoriums, the Asiad Games Village Complex and residential and commercial establishments fill the modern landscape between the Khel Gaon Marg and the Auro Bindo Marg in the heart of South Delhi.

Alaud'din is the best known of the Khalji dynasty because he extended his dominion to Southern India and established the second city of Delhi, Siri. He created Siri between 1297 and 1307 to defend against Mongol invasions of India and Delhi. In response he built Siri Fort, mimicked massive Turkish ones. The Fort served as the seat of his power during his campaigns to enlarge his territory. Due to frequent Mongolinvasions of West Asia, the Saljuqs took asylum in Delhi. The craftsmen of Seljuq dynasty are credited with this era's architectural monuments in Delhi.

Targhi, a Mongol ruler, besieged the Siri fort when Ala-ud-din Khalji retreated during the Mongol expedition into India. Targhi could not penetrate the fortifications of the Siri Fort and he finally retreated to his Kingdom in Central Asia. But this attack forced Allauddin to strengthen his defenses at the borders which enabled him to keep the Mongols away – Ali Beg and Tartaq and their army – after they attacked and plundered Punjab and Amroha. Alauddin deputed his two generals Ghazi Malik and Malik Kafur to repel the Mongol attack. The Mongol army was soundly beaten before they could return to Central Asia with their plunder; All the generals and soldiers of the Mongol army were captured and brought to Siri where they were trampled to death by elephants and decapitated.

The Mongols tried to attack one last time in 1306 AD but Ghazi Malik (who was the Governor of Punjab) annihilated the entire attacking Mongol army (believed to be 50,000 strong). Subsequent ruthless attacks by Allauddin's army, deep into Mongol territory in Kandahar, Ghazni and Kabul in Afghanistan ensured that Mongols would never attack India again. His military strategies were thus aimed at building an Indian Empire, which he had mostly succeeded. He consolidated his territory, ruled with military might for 20 years and was considered the "first real Emperor of India". Siri, which is now a part of New Delhi, was later linked to the fortifications of Jahanpanah. Siri was then also known as "Darul Khilafat" or "Seat of Califate" In 1398 AD, Timurlane, the Mongol ruler who invaded Delhi, wrote in his memoirs, " the Siri is a round city. Its buildings are lofty. They are surrounded by fortifications built of stone and brick, and they are very strong – from the fort of Siri to that of Old Delhi, which is a considerable distance – there runs a strong wall built of stone and cement. The part called Jahanpanah is situated in the midst of the inhabited city. The fortifications of the three cities (old Delhi, Siri and Tughlaqabad) have thirty gates. Jahanpanah has thirteen gates, Siri has seven gates. The fortifications of the Old Delhi have ten gates, some opening to the exterior and some towards the interior of the city."

According to the legend of Ala-ud-din's war exploits, the name Siri given to the Fort was because the foundation of the fort was built on the severed heads ('Siri' in Hindi means "head") of about 8,000 Mongol soldiers killed in the war. Another version of the legend refers to the war crimes committed by Allauddin when the Mongol army was defeated and the captured soldiers were brought to Siri and trampled by elephants, then their severed heads were hung on the walls of the Siri Fort.

Siri Fort was built 5 km (3.1 mi) to the north-east of the Qutab Minar on an old camp near Delhi. The first city is considered to be built by Muslims, it was in an oval shape; its ruins are presently seen in an area of about 1.7 km2 (0.7 sq mi).

Allauddin, the second ruler of the Khilji dynasty, laid the foundation for the City of Siri in 1303 AD. The structures built in Siri were stated to have had a fine imprint of the enthusiasm of the rulers of Khalji dynasty (particularly, the first three out of six Rulers of the Dynasty) with Allauddin's deep interests in architecture and his achievements supported by the imported skills of the artists of Saljuqs richly contributing to the efforts to build the new city. Legend states that Allauddin's prolific building involved engagement of 70,000 workers. The city was built with an oval plan with palaces and other structures.

There were seven gates for entry and exit, but at

present only the Southeastern gate exists. The fort was once considered the pride of the city for its palace of a thousand pillars called the Hazar Sutan. The palace was built outside the fort limits, and had marble floors and other stone decoration. Its Darwaza (door) is supposed to have been beautifully decorated. In eastern part of the ruins there are remnants of flame shaped battlements, loop holes for arrows, and bastions, which were considered unique new additions of that period. In the nearby Shahpur Jat village, some dilapidated structures of the period are seen. Tohfewala Gumbad Masjid (pictured) is one such structure whose ruins show the form of domed central apartment and sloping wall characteristic of Khaljis architecture.

Apart from building the Siri Fort, the citadel around it and the water supply system with a reservoir at Hauz Khas for providing water supply to Siri, his new city, Ala-ud-din also expanded the building activity around the religious city of the first city complex of Qutb complex by making additions to the Quwwatul-Islam Mosque, which doubled its original size, additions to the Qutub Minar itself (Nagari inscriptions on the tower attribute to this tower as *"Vijaya sthamba"* or victory tower of Ala-ud-din) and a grandiose plan of constructing a new Minar (tower) bigger (double) that of the Qutub Minar.

This plan was left half completed, as may be seen from the ruins at the site, due to the death of Allauddin in 1316. The destruction of the Fort is attributed to the local rulers who removed the fort's stones, bricks and other artifacts for their own buildings. In particular, Sher Shah Suri (1540–1545), of Pashtun Afghan descent from Eastern India (Bihar), took away material from Siri to build his own city. The battered walls of the fort had a wider base on the outside. A protected passage was provided within the battered walls (now seen in ruins as pictured).

The rest of the structures remained unexplored by Archeologists and these were unknowingly buried when the Asiad Village Complex was built in 1982 for the Asiad 1982. ASI has now launched an excavation programme, since December 2008, to unearth some portions of the wall concealed for centuries which will enable exposing the entire wall providing a continuous link with the earlier excavated stretches of the wall.

Asiad Village Complex

Near the ruins of the ancient fort city, the Asian Village Complex, popularly known as the Siri Fort Complex, was developed during the Asiad 1982 (the 1982 Asian Games) sports event. The complex was developed in the land around the Siri Fort ruins for the sports event involved. Among these buildings are a large sports complex of courts for tennis, badminton and basketball, a swimming pool, a golf course, gymnasium, aerobics centre, jogging tracks, cricket grounds, large auditoriums, upscale residential buildings, deluxe food joints and commercial establishments. This complex is now under further refurbishing and expansion for the 2010 Commonwealth Games, amidst protests and court interventions.

As part of beautifying the ancient monuments before the 2010 Commonwealth Games, the Archeological Survey of India (ASI), the custodians of heritage monuments in Delhi, have begun restoration works of several structures which includes the Siri Fort walls. According to their evaluation of three stretches of the fort walls, the first stretch nearer to the Asiad Village is in good shape, the second stretch next to the Panchsheel Park would need conservation actions costing Rs 50 lakhs and the third stretch next to the Asiad village needs conservation measures costing Rs 5 lakhs. In addition, the stretch adjoining Panchsheel Park, which has been evaluated as in a bad shape, has also been identified for undertaking restoration works at a cost of Rs 30 lakhs.

The Fort is located at the southern end of Hauz Khas and is 13 km (8.1 mi) from Delhi. It is approachable from Panchseel road in South Delhi. The road from Moolchand to Chirag Delhi passes through the middle of the fort precincts. An auditorium complex (three auditoriums) within the Siri Fort area run by the Government of India has a combined seating capacity of over 2,500. It is a prestigious entertainment centre in New Delhi where film festivals, dance performances, plays and music recitals are organized.

Moti Masjid

The Moti Masjid is a large white marble mosque built by the Mughal emperor Aurangzeb at the Red Fort complex in Delhi, India, from 1659-1660.

A mosque by the same name was also built in 1645 CE by Shah Jahan, Aurangzeb's father, inside the Lahore Fort in Lahore, Pakistan.

Another small mosque by the same name, was built for private prayer, by Mughal emperor, Bahadur Shah I (r. 1707-1712) and Aurangzeb's son, close to the *Ajmere Gate* of the dargah of Sufi saint, Qutbuddin Bakhtiar Kaki at Mehrauli, and is an imitation of the one inside the Red Fort of Delhi.

Shia Jama Masjid

Shia Jama Masjid is located at Kashmiri Gate, Delhi. Hujjatul-Islam Syed Ali Taqvi is it's Imam (prayer leader).

In Muharram one of the oldest processions is taken out from Shia Jama Masjid in Kashmiri Gate to Punja Sharif Karbala in the same locality.

Adham Khan's Tomb

Adham Khan's Tomb lies to the north of the Qutub Minar, Mehrauli, Delhi, immediately before one reaches the town of Mehrauli, built 1561, it is now a protected monument by Archeological Survey of India.

It lies on the walls of Lal Kot and rising from a terrace enclosed by an octagonal wall provided with low towers at the corners. It consists of a domed octagonal chamber in the Lodhi Dynasty style and Sayyid dynasty early in the 14th century. It has a verandah on each side pierced by three openings. It is known popularly as Bul-bulaiyan (a Labyrinth or Maze), for a visitor often loses his way amidst the several passages in the thickness of its walls.

Adham Khan, son of Maham Anga, a wet nurse of Akbar, was a nobleman and general in Akbar's army. In 1561, he fell out with Ataga Khan, Akbar's Prime Minister, and husband of Ji Ji Anga, another wet nurse, and killed him, whereupon he was thrown down from the ramparts of Agra Fort twice, by the order of the emperor Akbar and died

His mother after fortieth day of mourning also died out of grief, and both were buried in this tomb believed to be commissioned built by Akbar, in a conspicuous octagonal design, not seen in any Mughal building of that era, a designed perhaps designated to the traitors, as it was common design features visible in the tombs of the previous Sur Dynasty, and also the Lodhi dynasty now within in the present Lodhi Gardens (Delhi), which the Mughals considered traitors. In 1830s, a British officer named Blake of Bengal Civil Service, converted this tomb into his residential apartment and removed the graves to make way for his dining hall. Though the officer died soon, it continued to be used as a rest house for many years by the British, and at one point even as a police station and a post office.

The tomb was vacated and later restored by the orders of Lord Curzon, and the grave of Adham Khan has since been restored to the site, and lies right below the central dome, though that of his mother Maham Anga never was.

REFERENCES

"About Hauz Khas". http://delhitourismonline.com/hauzkhas.htm. Retrieved 2009-05-03.

Adham Khan's Tomb - Image and History *The New Cambridge History of India*, by Catherine B. Asher. Cambridge University Press.

Adham Khan's Tomb *Delhi*, by Patrick Horton, Richard Plunkett, Hugh Finlay. Lonely Planet, 2002, p. 127.

Adham Khan's Tomb *The Delhi that No-one Knows*, by R.V. Smith. Orient Longman, 2005.

Aitken, Bill (2001) [2002]. *Speaking Stones: World Cultural Heritage Sites in India*. Eicher Goodearth Limited. p. 23.

Alfred Frederick; Pollock Harcourt. *The New Guide to Delhi*. PaperbackshopUS. p. 79.

All About Delhi *Delhi, the Capital of India*, by Anon. Asian Educational Services, 1997.

Annual York-Noor Lecture Series: "Murder, Mausolea and the Emperor Akbar: Two Early Mughal Tombs" *York University*.

"Another wonder revealed: Qutub Minar draws most tourists, Taj a distant second". Indian Express. July 25, 2007.

Anon (1997). *Dictionary of Islamic architecture : Delhi, the capital of India*. Asian Educational Services. p. 62.

Anthony Welch. "A Medieveal Centre of Learning in India: The Hauz Khas Madrasa in Delhi -application" (pdf).

ASI have included the remaining unprotected monuments of Lodhi Garden under the Delhi Circle protection umbrella *The Hindu*, October 16, 2002.

Batra, N. L. (1996). *Heritage conservation: preservation and restoration of monuments*. Aryan Books International. p. 176.

Beyond the WALL The Hindu, September 25, 2003.

Chandra, Satish (2003). *History of architecture and ancient building materials in India*. Tech Books International. p. 107.

"Come rains, Hauz Khas lake will come alive". Delhi News line. 2004-03-23.

"Commonwealth Games-2010, Conservation, Restoration and Upgradation of Public Amenities at Protected Monuments" (pdf). *Red Fort & Salimgarh Fort*. Archeological Survey of India, Delhi Circle. 2006. pp. 37–38 & 40.

Delhi city guide, by Eicher Goodearth Limited, Delhi Tourism. Published by Eicher Goodearth Limited, 1998.

Dr. Akbar Ahmed. "The Trial of Dara Shikoh:A Play in Three Acts" (pdf). The Buxton Readings. p. 53.

Eicher:City Guide - Delhi, Eicher Goodearth Publication. 1998. ISBN 8190060120. *Page 117*

Fanshawe. H.C (1998). *Delhi, Past and Present*. Asian Educational Services. pp. 1 to 3.

Fatehpuri Shahi Masjid: A mute witness to the travails of Dillee milligazette. May 1, 2000.

Geraldine Forbes; Gordon Johnson, B. R. Tomlinson, Stewart Gordon, and Catherine Ella Blanshard Asher (1992). *The new Cambridge history of India*. Cambridge University Press. p. 10.

Gordon Sanderson; Maulvi Shuaib (2000). *Delhi Fort*. Asia Publication Services. pp. 80,81 & 82.

Hedger-Gourlay, Fiona coauthors = Lindy Ingham, Jo Newton, Emma Tabor and Jill Worrell (2006-09-13). "Lal Kot and Siri" (pdf).

History of Mughal Architecture, By R. Nath, Published by Abhinav Publications, 2006.

In memory of a pious Begum The Hindu, October 3, 2005.

Index_1200-1299: Qutb ud-Din Aibak and the Qubbat ul-Islam mosqueColumbia University.

Javeed, Tabassum (2008). *World Heritage Monuments and Related Edifices in India*. Algora Publishing. p. 107.

Kevin R. D. Shepherd. *A Sufi matriarch: Hazrat Babajaný*. Anthropographia Publications. p. 25.

Lucy Peck (2005). *Delhi - A thousand years of Building*. New Delhi: Roli Books Pvt Ltd.. pp. 135, 181, & 241.

Lucy Peck (2005). *Delhi - A thousand years of Building*. New Delhi: Roli Books Pvt Ltd.. pp. 87–89.

Lucy Peck (2005). *Delhi - A thousand years of Building*. New Delhi: Roli Books Pvt Ltd.. p. 46.

Lucy Peck (2005). *Delhi - A thousand years of Building*. New Delhi: Roli Books Pvt Ltd.. pp. 35, 44–45.

M H Syed (2004). *History of Delhi Sultanate*. Anmol Publications Pvt. Ltd.. p. 413.

Madan Mohan. "Historical Information System for Surveying Monuments and Spatial Data Modeling for Conservation of Cultural Heritage in Delhi" (pdf). pp. 5/16 & 5/17.

Maulana Hakim Saiyid Abdul Hai "Hindustan Islami Ahad Mein" (Hindustan under Islamic rule), Eng Trans by Maulana Abdul Hasan Nadwi.

Mohan, I.(1992). *The world of walled cities: conservation, environmental pollution, urban renewal and developmental prospects*. Mittal Publications. p. 23.

Mountstuart Elphinstone; Edward Byles Cowell (2006-06-27). *The History of India: The Hindú and Mahometan Periods*. Scientific Society (Aligarh, India),

Mughal Architecture of Delhi : A Study of Mosques and Tombs (1556-1627 A.D.), by Praduman K. Sharma, Sundeep, 2001.

Mughals *Dictionary of Islamic architecture*, by Andrew Petersen. Routledge, 1996.

Nath, R. (1978). *History of Sultanate architecture*. Abhinav Publications. p. 22.

"New Delhi - Hauz Khas Village". http://www.planetware.com/delhi/new-hauz-khas-village-ind-delhi-hauz.htm. Retrieved 2009-04-26.

Page, J.A. (1926) "An Historical Memoir on the Qutb, Delhi" *Memoirs of the Archaeological Society of India* 22: OCLC 5433409; republished (1970) Lakshmi Book Store, New Delhi.

Pankaj Tyagi. "Country's first tomb is victim of ASI's neglect". The Indian Muslim's Leading News Paper Milli Gazette.

Patrick Horton; , Richard Plunkett and Hugh Finlay (2002). *Delhi*. Lonely Planet. p. 232.

Poonam Bisht (2005-12-07). "A serious blow to Delhi's heritage as Army plans to build residential complex close to Sultan Garhi". Delhi Scoop.

Royal Mughal Ladies and Their Contributions By Soma Mukherjee, Published by Gyan Books, 2001.

S. Gajrani. *History, Religion and Culture of India*. p. 44.

Schimmel, Annemarie; Burzine K. Waghmar (2004). *The empire of the great Mughals*. Reaktion Books. p. 267.

Sharma, Y.D. (2001). *Delhi and its Neighbourhood*. New Delhi: Archeological Survey of India. pp. 22, 83–84.

Shiri Ram Bakshi (1995). *Delhi Through Ages*. Anmol Publications Pvt. Ltd.. pp. 70–71.

The Cambridge History of India: Mughal Period, by Edward James Rapson. Published by University Press, 1937. *Page 532 Tomb of Adham Khan*.

The History of the Taj and the Buildings in Its Vicinity: With 3 Illustrations from Photographs and 2 Plans, By Muhammad Mu»în al-Dîn, Akbarâbâdî Mu#ammad Mu»în al-Dîn Published by Moon press, 1905.

Walk with royalty Business Line, February 23, [[2007].

World Heritage Sites - Humayun's Tomb: Characteristics of Indo-Islamic architecture Archaeological Survey of India (ASI).

"World Heritage Monuments and Related Edifices in India". *Pg.107*. Google Books.

8

Stadiums in Delhi

For different sports different specious and well equipped stadiums are necessary. Though Delhi has already hosted Asian Games in 1982, for ensuing Commonwealth Games 2010 Delhi has renovated its stadiums. Here in this chapter we will put light on different stadiums in Delhi.

1. JAWAHARLAL NEHRU STADIUM, DELHI

The Jawaharlal Nehru Stadium in Delhi, India, was built by the Government of India in 1982.This stadium is named after the first prime minister of India. The massive facility is an all-purpose sports arena hosting football (soccer) and other sporting events, as well as large-scale entertainment events, such as concerts by India's leading musical acts and entertainers. The facility seats 78,000 spectators, and up to 130,000 for concerts. In terms of sitting capacity, it is the third biggest stadium in India and the 57th largest in the world. The stadium also houses the headquarters of the Indian Olympic Association. The Jawaharlal Nehru Stadium was first constructed to host the 9th Asian Games in 1982 (India had also hosted the first Games in 1951, also in New Delhi). The stadium will also host the upcoming 2010 Commonwealth Games.

In preparation for the Games, the stadium is undergoing a refurbishment that will reduce the capacity to 60-75,000 spectators. It will be completed in early 2010.

Cricket Matches

The Stadium has hosted two One Day International matches featuring India: against Australia in 1984, and South Africa in 1991. Batsman Kepler Wessels played in both the matches, but for different countries, scoring 107 for Australia and 90 for South Africa.

Renovation

The Jawaharlal Nehru Stadium is being given a face lift with a new roof and improved seating and other facilities to meet international standards when it hosts the opening and closing ceremonies as well as the Athletics Events during the XIX Commonwelath Games, which are to be held in Delhi from October 3 - 14, 2010 in Delhi.

The 53,800 sq m Teflon-coated roof, designed by Schlaich Bergermann & Partner is being built at a cost of Rs. 308 crore. It covers an area of 100 acres.

Two new venues are being constructed next to the stadium for the Games: Four synthetic greens for the Lawn Bowls event and a 2,500-seat gymnasium for the weightlifting event. A 400-metre warm-up track will also be constructed. 150m long tunnel is being constructed for the opening and closing ceremonies.

The support structure for the new roof has apparently made the stadium look like a completely permanent version of London's Olympic Stadium.

2. DHYAN CHAND NATIONAL STADIUM

Dhyan Chand National Stadium is a field hockey stadium

at New Delhi, India. It originally held 25,000 people. It is named after former famous Indian field hockey player, Dhyan Chand. The national stadium Is also well known for its Cricket coaching. The Dronacharya Award winner for Cricket, Sunita Sharma coaches cricket at this facility. It served as the venue for the 1st Asian Games in 1951. A 50-metre swimming pool is built to the east of the stadium.

Remarkably, the stadium was originally built in 1933 as a multipurpose stadium and named the Irwin Amphitheatre. It was designed by Anthony S. DeMillo. It was renamed National Stadium before the 1951 Asian Games, Dhyan Chand's name was added in 2002.

Major Renovations

The Dhyan Chand Stadium is the host venue for the 2010 Men's Hockey World Cup. It will also be the hockey venue of the 2010 Commonwealth Games. The stadium underwent a major reconstruction project before the Hockey World Cup 2010.

On 24th January 2010 it became the first venue for the 2010 Commonwealth Games to be unveiled. The stadium was revamped at a cost of Rs 266 crore. The original stands, which were earthen embankments, were demolished and a new rectangular seating bowl was constructed in its place.

Main Features

The stadium is spread over 17,500 square metres in the 37-acre complex. It has three synthetic pitches — two conform to international standards and a third is for practice.

A new polygrass turf was laid on all pitches equipped with new sprinkler systems. The main field has a capacity to seat about 16,200 spectators. The second pitch outside the main arena has 900 permanent seats and with a provision of 1,600 temporary seats.The two competitive pitches are flood-lit with foldable floodlight towers (hinged mast lights) which will provide 2,200 lux illumination during the competition. This will enable high definition TV transmission.

In fact, the stadium has state-of-the-art sound system with required acoustic effects and also two scoreboards on right and left flanks overlooking the spectators' areas. Both the pitches are equipped with state-of-the-art facilities for the players like change rooms, relaxation lounges and a spacious VVIP lounge. The entire stadium is centrally air-conditioned and fitted with lifts, barrier free provisions for athletes and spectators who are physically challenged. The stadium will get its power supply from two grids with a backup based on generator sets and battery uninterrupted power supply.

3. INDIRA GANDHI ARENA

The Indira Gandhi Arena, located at the Indraprastha Estate in the eastern region of New Delhi, is the largest indoor sports arena in India and the second-largest in Asia and the World. Built by the Government of India in 1982 in order to host the indoor games events in the Asiad Games, the arena's grounds cover an area of 102 acres. Since its construction, the arena hosted a number of other tournaments as well. The facility seats 25,000 people and is named after former Prime Minister of India Indira Gandhi.

Since its inception, the arena has been repeatedly renovated and modernized. Equipped with soundproof synthetics walls, lighting systems, and audio system, the arena will undergo another round of renovation to prepare it for the 2010 Commonwealth Games. Renovation is scheduled to be completed December 31, 2009.

It has been renovated for the 2010 Commonwealth Games at a cost of Rs. 240 crore.

4. THYAGARAJ SPORTS COMPLEX

Thyagaraj Sport Complex is a sports stadium in New Delhi. The Thyagaraj Sports Complex is a model Green Stadium with world class facilities in India. Constructed over an area of 16.5 acres and a capacity of 4,494, the Thyagaraj Stadium was built with the latest green building technologies such as the use of fly ash bricks in construction. The stadium will feature effective water management systems such as rainwater harvesting, sewage treatment with a capacity of 200,000 litres per day, dual flush systems, sensor-based faucets etc. Innovative landscaping is being done with an emphasis on native species and reduction in soil toxicity. It was built from scratch at a cost of Rs. 300 crore.

In terms of energy efficiency, the Thyagaraj Stadium will be setting a benchmark. Lighting will be done using solar energy. In addition, building-integrated photovoltaic concept will be implemented. So, the stadium will start feeding electricity to the grid. It has the capacity 4495.

Facilities One match court; two warm-up courts

Commonwealth Games 2010

The Thyagaraj Stadium is a venue for Netball during the 2010 Commonwealth Games.

5. SIRI FORT SPORTS COMPLEX

Siri Fort Sport Complex is a sports stadium in New Delhi.

Badminton

Capacity 4748

Facilities Five match courts; three warm-up courts

Squash

Capacity 3128

Facilities 11 singles courts (convertible into five doubles courts)

2010 Commonwealth Games

The stadium will host the sports Badminton and Squash for the Games. The Stadium for Badminton will have five match courts and three warm-up courts, and the Stadium for Squash will have 11 singles courts convertible to five doubles courts.

6. DR. KARNI SINGH SHOOTING RANGE

Dr. Karni Singh Shooting Range is a shooting range in New Delhi.It was constructed for the 1982 Asian Games in New Delhi. It is also a venue for the 2010 Commonwealth Games and for that it underwent rebuilding and all the facilities were enhanced and now the venue boasts of the most enhanced facilities in the world.

In October 2008 the structure of the range was fully demolished and was built under a project a plan costing Rs. 150 crore, it was completed in 13 months. Spread over 72 acres, the Range has been divided into six parts — a 10-metre range, a 25-metre range, a 50-metre range, a final range, trap and skeet range and a new armoury building which were constructed with state-of-the-art technology.

The earlier separate ranges for Trap and Skeet were converted into new composite ranges for Trap and Skeet with state-of-the-art scoring equipments. For the 10-metre shooting range, a centrally air-conditioned indoor facility with complete power back-up was constructed with a capacity of maximum of 500 spectators. Two different grids will be providing electricity to ensure complete power back-up. The 25-metre shooting range is an outdoor venue with only the seating area covered; the shooter though has shade on his head. There are 50 firing points for this range.

The rebuilding of the site was followed by massive plantation and beautification would to make the site more attractive. There are also plans for constructing a 200-seated hostel which will be a self-contained facility to help the campers.

7. TALKATORA STADIUM

Talkatora Indoor Stadium is a indoor stadium located in New Delhi. The stadium has a capacity of 3035 peeople. The Stadium will have one competition ring and four warm-up areas. The Stadium will also have a tunnel to facilitate movement of the athletes from the Facility Block to the main stadium.

The stadium is a venue for the 2010 Commonwealth Games for the event of boxing.

8. SPM SWIMMING POOL COMPLEX

Dr. S.P. Mukherjee Swimming Stadium or SPM Swimming Pool Complex is a swimming complex in New Delhi that is undergoing construction for the 2010 Commonwealth Games.

Facilities

- One competition pool

- One diving pool
- One warm-up pool

2010 Commonwealth Games

The stadium is a venue for the 2010 Commonwealth Games for the events of aquatics.

Appendices

As mega events like Commonwealth Games put great pressure on logistics environment, it is pertinent to know the laws enacted for environment protection. The text of some such laws is reproduced below for the benefit of readers.

APPENDIX—I

THE ENVIRONMENT (PROTECTION) ACT, 1986

MINISTRY OF ENVIRONMENT & FORESTS GOVERNMENT OF INDIA

NO. 29 TO 1986

(23rd May, 1986)

An Act to provide for the protection and improvement of environment and for matters connected there with:

Whereas the decisions were taken at the United NationsConference on the Human Environment held at Stockholm in June, 1972, in which India participated, to take appropriate steps for the protection and improvement of human environment;

And whereas it is considered necessary further to implement the decisions aforesaid in so far as they relate to the protection and improvement of environment and the prevention of hazards to human beings, other living creatures, plants and property;

Be it enacted by Parliament in the Thirty-seventh Year of the Republic of India as follows:-

CHAPTER I

PRELIMINARY

1.Short Title, Extent and Commencement

(1) This Act may be Called the Environment (Protection) Act, 1986.

(2) It extends to the whole of India.

(3) It shall come into force on such date as the Central Government may, by notification in the Official Gazette, appoint and different dates may be appointed for different provisions of this Act and for different areas.[1]

2. Definitions

In this Act, unless the context otherwise requires,—

(a) "environment" includes water, air and land and the inter-relationship which exists among and between water, air and land, and human beings, other living creatures, plants, micro-organism and property;

(b) "environmental pollutant" means any solid, liquid or gaseous substance present in such concentration as may be, or tend to be, injurious to environment;

(c) "environmental pollution" means the presence in the environment of any environmental pollutant;

(d) "handling", in relation to any substance, means the manufacture, processing, treatment, package, storage, transportation, use, collection, destruction, conversion, offering for sale, transfer or the like of such substance;

(e) "hazardous substance" means any substance or preparation which, by reason of its chemical or physico-chemical properties or handling, is liable to cause harm to human beings, other living creatures, plant, micro-organism, property or the environment;

(f) "occupier", in relation to any factory or premises, means a person who has, control over the affairs of the factory or the premises and includes in relation to any substance, the person in possession of the substance;

(g) "prescribed" means prescribed by rules made under this Act.

CHAPTER II

GENERAL POWERS OF THE CENTRAL GOVERNMENT

3. Power of Central Government to Take Measures to Protect and Improve Environment

(1) Subject to the provisions of this Act, the Central Government, shall have the power to take all such measures as it deems necessary or expedient for the purpose of protecting and improving the quality of the environment and preventing controlling and abating environmental pollution.

(2) In particular, and without prejudice to the generality of the provisions of sub-section (1), such measures may include measures with respect to all or any of the following matters, namely:

(i) co-ordination of actions by the State Governments, officers and other authorities—

(a) under this Act, or the rules made thereunder, or

(b) under any other law for the time being in force which is relatable to the objects of this Act;

(ii) planning and execution of a nation-wide programme for the prevention, control and abatement of environmental pollution;

(iii) laying down standards for the quality of environment in its various aspects;

(iv) laying down standards for emission or discharge of environmental pollutants from various sources whatsoever:

Provided that different standards for emission or discharge may be laid down under this clause from different sources having regard to the quality or composition of the emission or discharge of environmental pollutants from such sources;

(v) restriction of areas in which any industries, operations or processes or class of industries, operations or processes shall not be carried out or shall be carried out subject to certain safeguards;

(vi) laying down procedures and safeguards for the prevention of accidents which may cause environmental pollution and remedial measures for such accidents;

(vii) laying down procedures and safeguards for the handling of hazardous substances;

(viii) examination of such manufacturing processes, materials and substances as are likely to cause environmental pollution;

(ix) carrying out and sponsoring investigations and research relating to problems of environmental pollution;

(x) inspection of any premises, plant, equipment, machinery, manufacturing or other processes, materials or substances and giving, by order, of such directions to such authorities, officers or persons as it may consider necessary to take steps for the prevention, control and abatement of environmental pollution;

(xi) establishment or recognition of environmental laboratories and institutes to carry out the functions entrusted to such environmental laboratories and institutes under this Act;

(xii) collection and dissemination of information in respect of matters relating to environmental pollution;

(xiii) preparation of manuals, codes or guides relating to the prevention, control and abatement of environmental pollution;

(xiv) such other matters as the Central Government deems necessary or expedient for the purpose of securing the effective implementation of the provisions of this Act.

(3) The Central Government may, if it considers it necessary or expedient so to do for the purpose of this Act, by order, published in the Official Gazette, constitute an authority or authorities by such name or names as may be specified in the order for the purpose of exercising and performing such of the powers and functions (including the power to issue directions under section 5) of the Central Government under this Act and for taking measures with respect to such of the matters referred to in sub-section (2) as may be mentioned in the order and subject to the supervision and control of the Central Government and the provisions of such order, such authority or authorities may exercise and powers or perform the functions or take the measures so mentioned in the order as if such authority or authorities had been empowered by this Act to exercise those powers or perform those functions or take such measures.

4. Appontment of Officers and Their Powers and Functions

(1) Without prejudice to the provisions of sub-section (3) of section 3, the Central Government may appoint officers with such designation as it thinks fit for the purposes of this Act and may entrust to them such of the powers and functions under this Act as it may deem fit.

(2) The officers appointed under sub-section (1) shall be subject to the general control and direction of the Central Government or, if so directed by that Government, also of the authority or authorities, if any, constituted under sub- section (3) of section 3 or of any other authority or officer.

5. Power to Give Directions

Notwithstanding anything contained in any other law but subject to the provisions of this Act, the Central Government[2] may, in the exercise of its powers and performance of its functions under this Act, issue directions in writing to any person, officer or any authority and such person, officer or authority shall be bound to comply with such directions.[3]

Explanation—For the avoidance of doubts, it is hereby declared that the power to issue directions under this section includes the power to direct—

(a) the closure, prohibition or regulation of any industry, operation or process; or

(b) stoppage or regulation of the supply of electricity or water or any other service.

6. Rules to Regulate Environment Pollution

(1) The Central Government may, by notification in the Official Gazette, make rules in respect of all or any of the matters referred to in section 3.

(2) In particular, and without prejudice to the generality of the foregoing power, such rules may provide for all or any of the following matters, namely:—

  (a) the standards of quality of air, water or soil for various areas and purposes;[4]

  (b) the maximum allowable limits of concentration of various environmental pollutants (including noise) for different areas;

  (c) the procedures and safeguards for the handling of hazardous substances;[5]

(d) the prohibition and restrictions on the handling of hazardous substances in different areas;[6]

(e) the prohibition and restriction on the location of industries and the carrying on process and operations in different areas;[7]

(f) the procedures and safeguards for the prevention of accidents which may cause environmental pollution and for providing for remedial measures for such accidents.[8]

CHAPTER III

PREVENTION, CONTROL, AND ABATEMENT OF ENVIRONMENTAL POLLUTION

7. Persons Carrying on Industry Operation, Etc., Not to Allow Emission or Discharge of Environmental Pollutants in Excess of the Standards

No person carrying on any industry, operation or process shall discharge or emit or permit to be discharged or emitted any environmental pollutants in excess of such standards as may be prescribed.[9]

8. Persons Handling Hazardous Substances to Comply with Procedural Safeguards

No person shall handle or cause to be handled any hazardous substance except in accordance with such procedure and after complying with such safeguards as may be prescribed.[10]

9. Furnishing of Information to Authorities and Agencies in Certain Cases

(1) Where the discharge of any environmental pollutant in excess of the prescribed standards occurs or is

apprehended to occur due to any accident or other unforeseen act or event, the person responsible for such discharge and the person in charge of the place at which such discharge occurs or is apprehended to occur shall be bound to prevent or mitigate the environmental pollution caused as a result of such discharge and shall also forthwith—

(a) intimate the fact of such occurrence or apprehension of such occurrence; and

(b) be bound, if called upon, to render all assistance, to such authorities or agencies as may be prescribed.[11]

(2) On receipt of information with respect to the fact or apprehension on any occurrence of the nature referred to in sub-section (1), whether through intimation under that sub-section or otherwise, the authorities or agencies referred to in sub-section (1) shall, as early as practicable, cause such remedial measures to be taken as necessary to prevent or mitigate the environmental pollution.

(3) The expenses, if any, incurred by any authority or agency with respect to the remedial measures referred to in sub-section (2), together with interest (at such reasonable rate as the Government may, by order, fix) from the date when a demand for the expenses is made until it is paid, may be recovered by such authority or agency from the person concerned as arrears of land revenue or of public demand.

10. Powers of Entry and Inspection

(1) Subject to the provisions of this section, any person empowered by the Central Government in this

behalf[12] shall have a right to enter, at all reasonable times with such assistance as he considers necessary, any place—

(a) for the purpose of performing any of the functions of the Central Government entrusted to him;

(b) for the purpose of determining whether and if so in what manner, any such functions are to be performed or whether any provisions of this Act or the rules made thereunder orany notice, order, direction or authorisation served, made, given or granted under this Act is being or has been complied with;

(c) for the purpose of examining and testing any equipment, industrial plant, record, register, document or any other material object or for conducting a search of any building in which he has reason to believe that an offence under this Act or the rules made thereunder has been or is being or is about to be committed and for seizing any such equipment, industrial plant, record, register, document or other material object if he has reason to believe that it may furnish evidence of the commission of an offence punishable under this Act or the rules made thereunder or that such seizure is necessary to prevent or mitigate environmental pollution.

(2) Every person carrying on any industry, operation or process of handling any hazardous substance shall be bound to render all assistance to the person empowered by the Central Government under sub-section (1) for carrying out the functions under that sub-section and if he fails to do so

without any reasonable cause or excuse, he shall be guilty of an offence under this Act.

(3) If any person wilfully delays or obstructs any persons empowered by the Central Government under sub-section (1) in the performance of his functions, he shall be guilty of an offence under this Act.

(4) The provisions of the Code of Criminal Procedure, 1973, or, in relation to the State of Jammu and Kashmir, or an area in which that Code is not in force, the provisions of any corresponding law in force in that State or area shall, so far as may be, apply to any search or seizures under this section as they apply to any search or seizure made under the authority of a warrant issued under section 94 of the said Code or as the case may be, under the corresponding provision of the said law.

11. Power to Take Simple and Procedure to be Followed in Connection Therewith

(1) The Central Government or any officer empowered by it in this behalf,[13] shall have power to take, for the purpose of analysis, samples of air, water, soil or other substance from any factory, premises or other place in such manner as may be prescribed.[14]

(2) The result of any analysis of a sample taken under sub-section (1) shall not be admissible in evidence in any legal proceeding unless the provisions of sub-sections (3) and (4) are complied with.

(3) Subject to the provisions of sub-section (4), the person taking the sample under sub-section (1) shall—

(a) serve on the occupier or his agent or person in charge of the place, a notice, then and there, in such form as may be prescribed, of his intention to have it so analysed;

(b) in the presence of the occupier of his agent or person, collect a sample for analysis;

(c) cause the sample to be placed in a container or containers which shall be marked and sealed and shall also be signed both by the person taking the sample and the occupier or his agent or person;

(d) send without delay, the container or the containers to the laboratory established or recognised by the Central Government under section 12.

(4) When a sample is taken for analysis under sub-section (1) and the person taking the sample serves on the occupier or his agent or person, a notice under clause (a) of sub-section (3), then,—

(a) in a case where the occupier, his agent or person wilfully absents himself, the person taking the sample shall collect the sample for analysis to be placed in a container or containers which shall be marked and sealed and shall also be signed by the person taking the sample, and

(b) in a case where the occupier or his agent or person present at the time of taking the sample refuses to sign the marked and sealed container or containers of the sample as required under clause (c) of sub-section (3), the marked and sealed container or containers shall be signed by the person taking the samples, and the container or containers shall be sent without delay by the person taking the sample for analysis to the laboratory established or recognised under section 12 and such person shall inform the Government Analyst appointed or recognised under section 13 in writing, about the wilfull absence of the occupier or his agent or person, or, as the case may be, his refusal to sign the container or containers.

12.Environmental Laboratories

(1) The Central Government[15] may, by notification in the Official Gazette,—

(a) establish one or more environmental laboratories;

(b) recognise one or more laboratories or institutes as environmental laboratories to carry out the functions entrusted to an environmental laboratory under this Act.[16]

(2) The Central Government may, by notification in the Official Gazette, make rules specifying—

(a) the functions of the environmental laboratory;[17]

(b) the procedure for the submission to the said laboratory of samples of air, water, soil or other substance for analysis or tests, the form of the laboratory report thereon and the fees payable for such report;[18]

(c) such other matters as may be necessary or expedient to enable that laboratory to carry out its functions.

13. Government Analysis

The Central Government may by notification in the Official Gazette, appoint or recognise such persons as it thinks fit and having the prescribed qualifications[19] to be Government Analysts for the purpose of analysis of samples of air, water, soil or other substance sent for analysis to any environmental laboratory established or recognised under sub-section (1) of section 12.

14. Reports of Government Analysts

Any document purporting to be a report signed by a Government analyst may be used as evidence of the facts stated therein in any proceeding under this Act.

15. Penalty for Contravention of the Provisions of the Act and Rules, Orders and Directions

(1) Whoever fails to comply with or contravenes any of the provisions of this Act, or the rules made or orders or directions issued thereunder, shall, in respect of each such failure or contravention, be punishable with imprisonment for a term which may extend to five years with fine which may extend to one lakh rupees, or with both, and in case the failure or contravention continues, with additional fine which may extend to five thousand rupees for every day during which such failure or contravention continues after the conviction for the first such failure or contravention.

(2) If the failure or contravention referred to in sub section (1) continues beyond a period of one year after the date of conviction, the offender shall be punishable with imprisonment for a term which may extend to seven years.

16. Offences by Companies

(1) Where any offence under this Act has been committed by a company, every person who, at the time the offence was committed, was directly

in charge of, and was responsible to, the company for the conduct of the business of the company, as well as the company, shall be deemed to be guilty of the offence and shall be liable to be proceeded against and punished accordingly:

Provided that nothing contained in this sub-section shall render any such person liable to any punishment provided in this Act, if he proves that the offence was committed without his knowledge or that he exercised all due diligence to prevent the commission of such offence.

(2) Notwithstanding anything contained in sub-section (1), where an offence under this Act has been committed by a company and it is proved that the offence has been committed with the consent or connivance of, or is attributable to any neglect on the part of, any director, manager, secretary or other officer of the company, such director, manager, secretary or other officer shall also deemed to be guilty of that offence and shall be liable to be proceeded against and punished accordingly.

Explanation—For the purpose of this section,—

(a) "company" means any body corporate and includes a firm or other association of individuals;

(b) "director", in relation to a firm, means a partner in the firm.

17. Offences by Government Department

(1) Where an offence under this Act has been committed by any Department of Government, the Head of the Department shall be deemed to be guilty of

the offence and shall be liable to be proceeded against and punished accordingly:

Provided that nothing contained in this section shall render such Head of the Department liable to any punishment if he proves that the offence was committed without his knowledge or that he exercise all due diligence to prevent the commission of such offence.

(2) Notwithstanding anything contained in sub-section (1), where an offence under this Act has been committed by a Department of Government and it is proved that the offence has been committed with the consent or connivance of, or is attributable to any neglect on the part of, any officer, other than the Head of the Department, such officer shall also be deemed to be guilty of that offence and shall be liable to be proceeded against and punished accordingly.

CHAPTER IV

MISCELLANEOUS

18. Protection of Action Taken in Good Faith

No suit, prosecution or other legal proceeding shall lie against the Government or any officer or other employee of the Government or any authority constituted under this Act or any member, officer or other employee of such authority in respect of anything which is done or intended to be done in good faith in pursuance of this Act or the rules made or orders or directions issued thereunder.

19. Cognizance of Offences

No court shall take cognizance of any offence under this Act except on a complaint made by—

(a) the Central Government or any authority or officer authorised in this behalf by that Government,[20] or

(b) any person who has given notice of not less than sixty days, in the manner prescribed, of the alleged offence and of his intention to make a complaint, to the Central Government or the authority or officer authorised as aforesaid.

20. Information, Reports or Returns

The Central Government may, in relation to its function under this Act, from time to time, require any person, officer, State Government or authority to furnish to it or any statistics, accounts and other information and such person, officer, State Government or other authority shall be bound to do so.

21. Members, Officers and Employees of the Authority Constituted Under Section 3 to be Public Servants

All the members of the authority, constituted, if any, in pursuance of any provisions of this Act or the rules made or orders or directions issued thereunder shall be deemed to be public servants within the meaning of section 21 of the Indian Penal Code (45 of 1860).

22. Bar of Jurisdiction

No civil court shall have jurisdiction to entertain any suit or proceeding in respect of anything done, action taken or order or direction issued by the Central Government or any other authority or officer in pursuance of any power conferred by or in relation to its or his functions under this Act.

23. Powers to Delegate

Without prejudice to the provisions of sub-section (3) of section 3, the Central Government may, by notification in the Official Gazette, delegate, subject to such conditions and limitations as may be specified in the notifications, such of its powers and functions under this Act [except the powers to constitute an authority under sub-section (3) of section 3 and to make rules under section 25] as it may deem necessary or expedient, to any officer, State Government or other authority.

24. Effect of Other Laws

(1) Subject to the provisions of sub-section (2), the provisions of this Act and the rules or orders made therein shall have effect notwithstanding anything inconsistent therewith contained in any enactment other than this Act.

(2) Where any act or omission constitutes an offence punishable under this Act and also under any other Act then the offender found guilty of such offence shall be liable to be punished under the other Act and not under this Act.

25. Power to Make Rules

(1) The Central Government may, by notification in the Official Gazette, make rules for carrying out the purposes of this Act.

(2) In particular, and without prejudice to the generality of the foregoing power, such rules may provide for all or any of the following matters, namely—

(a) the standards in excess of which environmental pollutants shall not be discharged or emitted under section 7;[21]

(b) the procedure in accordance with and the safeguards in compliance with which hazardous substances shall be handled or caused to be handled under section 8;[22]

(c) the authorities or agencies to which intimation of the fact of occurrence or apprehension of occurrence of the discharge of any environmental pollutant in excess of the prescribed standards shall be given and to whom all assistance shall be bound to be rendered under sub-section (1) of section 9;[23]

(d) the manner in which samples of air, water, soil or other substance for the purpose of analysis shall be taken under sub-section (1) of section 11;[24]

(e) the form in which notice of intention to have a sample analysed shall be served under clause (a) of sub section (3) of section 11;[25]

(f) the functions of the environmental laboratories,[26] the procedure for the submission to such laboratories of samples of air, water, soil and other substances for analysis or test;[27] the form of laboratory report; the fees payable for such report and other matters to enable such laboratories to carry out their functions under sub-section (2) of section 12;

(g) the qualifications of Government Analyst appointed or recognised for the purpose of analysis of samples of air, water, soil or other substances under section 13;[28]

(h) the manner in which notice of the offence

and of the intention to make a complaint to the Central Government shall be given under clause (b) of section 19;[29]

(i) the authority of officer to whom any reports, returns, statistics, accounts and other information shall be furnished under section 20;

(j) any other matter which is required to be, or may be, prescribed.

26. Rules Made Under This Act to be Laid Before Parliament

Every rule made under this Act shall be laid, as soon as may be after it is made, before each Hose of Parliament, while it is in session, for a total period of thirty days which may be comprised in one session or in two or more successive sessions, and if, before the expiry of the session immediately following the session or the successive sessions aforesaid, both Houses agree in making any modification in the rule or both Houses agree that the rule should not be made, the rule shall thereafter have effect only in such modified form or be of no effect, as the case may be; so, however, that any such modification or annulment shall be without prejudice to the validity of anything previously done under that rule.

REFERENCES

1. It came into force in the whole of India on 19th November, 1986 vide Notification No. G.S.R. 1198(E) dated 12-11-86 published in the Gazette of India No. 525 dated 12-11-86.
2. The Central Government has delegated the powers vested m it under section 5 of the Act to the State Governments of Andhra Pradesh, Assam, Bihar, Gujarat, Haryana, Himachal Pradesh, Karnatalca, Kerala, Madhya Predesh, Mizoram, Orissa, Rajasthan, Sikkim and Tamil Nadu subject to the

condition that the Central Government may revoke such delegation of powers in respect of all or any one or more of the State Governments or may itself invoke the provisions of section 5 of the Act, if in the opinion of the Central Government such a course of action is necessary in public interest, (Notification No, S.O. 152 (E) dated 10-2-88 published in Gazette No. 54 of the same date). These Powers have been delegated to the following State Governments also on the same terms:

Meghalaya, Punjab and Uttar Pradesh vide Notification No. S.0.389 (E) dated 14-4-88 published in the Gazette No. 205 dated 144-88;

Maharashtra vide Notification No. S.O. 488(E) dated 17-5-88 published in the Gazette No. 255 dated 17-5-88;

Goa and Jammu & Kashmir vide Notification No. S.O. 881 (E) dated 22-9-88; published in the Gazette No. 749 dated 22.9.88.

West Bengal Manipur vide Notificadon N. S.O. 408 (E) dated 6-6-89; published in the Gazette No. 319 dated 6-6-89;

Tripura vide Notification No. S.O. 479 (E) dated 25-7-91 published in thc Gazene No. 414 dated 25-7-91.

3. For issuing directions see r.4 of Enviromnent (Protection) Rules, 1986.

4. See r. 3 of Environment (Protection) Rules, 1986 and Schedules thereto.

   i. Schedule I lists the standards for emission or discharge of environmental pollutants from the industries, processes or operations and their maximum allowable limits of concentration;

   ii. Schedule II lists general standards for discharge of effluents and their maximum limits of concentration allowable;

   iii. Schedule III lists ambient air quality standards in respect of noise and its maximum allowable limits; and

   iv. Schedule IV lists standards for emission of smoke, vapour etc. from motor vehicles and maximum allowable limits of their emission.

5. See r. 13 of Environment (Protection) Rules, 1986, and

i. Hazardous Wastes (Management and Handling) Rules, 1989;

ii. Manufacture, Storage and Import of Hazardous Chemicals Rules, 1989; and

iii. Rules for the Manufacture, Use, Import, Export and Storage of Hazardous Micro organisms, Genetically-engineered organisms or Cells.

6. Rule 13 SUPRA.

7. See r. 5 of Environment (Protection) Rules, 1986.

8. See r. 12 of Environment (Protection) Rules and Schedule 11, and relevant provisions of Hazardous Wastes (Management and Handling) Rules, Manufacture, Storage and Import of Hazardous Chemicals Rules and Rules for the Manufacture, Use, Import Export and Storage of hazardous Micro-organisms, Genetically Engineered Organisms or Cells.

9. See r. 3 of Environment (Protection) Rules, 1486 and Schedule I.

10. See r. 13 of Environment (Protection) Rules, 1986 and

    i. Hazardous Wastes (Management and Handling) Rules, 1989;

    ii. Manufacture, Storage and Import of Hazardous Chemicals Rules, 1989; and

    iii. Rules for the Manufacture, Use Import, Export and Storage of Hazardous Micro organisms, Genetically Engineered organisms or Cells.

11. For authorities or agencies see r. 12 of Environment (Protection) Rules, 1986 and Schedule II.

12. The Central Govt. has empowered 60 persons listed in the Table (p. 251) vide S.O. 83 (E) published in the Gazette of India No. 66 dated 16-2-87 and S.O. 63 (E) published in the Gazette of India No. 42 dated 18-1-88.

13. In excercise of powers conferred under sub-section (i) of section 11 the Central Government has empowered 60 officers listed in the Table (p. 254) vide S.O. 84. (E) published in the Gazette No. 66 dated 16-2-87 and S.O. 62(E) published in the Gazette No. 42 dated 18-1-88.

14. For procedure for taking samples see r. 6 of Environment (Protection) Rules, 1986, also.
15. The Central Government has delegated its powers under clause (b) of sub-section (i) of section 12 and section 13 of the Act to the Central Pollution Control Board vide Notification No. S.O. 145 (E) dated 21-2-91 published in the Gazette No. 128 dated 27-2-91.
16. The list of laboratories/institutes recognised as environmental laboratories: and the persons recognised as Govt. Analysts is given in the table (p. 223).
17. See r. 9 of Environment (Protection) Rules, 1986.
18. See r. 8 of Environment (Protection) Rules, 1986.
19. For qualification of Govt. Analyst sec. r. 10 of Environment (Protection) Rules, 1986.
20. In exercise of powers conferred under clause (a) of section 19, the Central-Government has authorised the officers and authorities vide S.O. 394 (E) published in the Gazette No. 185 dated 16-4-87, S.O. 237(E) published in the Gazette No. 171 dated 29-3-89 published in the Gazette No. 519 dated 21-8-89.
21. See footnote 2 on Page 213.
22. See footnote 3 on Page 213.
23. See footnote I on Page 214.
24. See r.6 of Environment (Protection) Rules, 1986.
25. See r. 7 of Environment (Protection) Rules, 1986.
26. See r. 9 of Environment (Protection) Rules, 1986.
27. For the procedure for submission of samples to laboratories and the form of laboratory report see r. 8 of Environment (Protection) Rules, 1986.
28. See r. 10 of Environment (Protection) Rules, 1986.
29. See r. 11 of Environment (protection) Rules, 1986.

APPENDIX—II

TOURISM IN INDIA: USEFUL LINKS

Airlines

Air India

http://www.airindia.com//

Indian Airlines

http://indian-airlines.nic.in/

Jet Airways

http://www.jetairways.com/

Aerofloat

http://www.aeroflot.org/

Air France

http://www.airfrance.com/

Air Lanka

http://www.srilankan.lk/

Air Canada

http://www.aircanada.ca/

All Nippon airways

http://svc.ana.co.jp/eng/index.html

Austrian Airlines

http://www.aua.com/

Biman Bangladesh Airlines

http://www.bangladeshonline.com/biman/

British Airways
http://www.britishairways.com/

Cathay Pacific
http://www.cathaypacific.com/

EL AL Israel Airlines
http://www.elal.co.il/

Ethiopian Airlines
http://www.toursundtravel.de/ethiopian-airlines.htm

Emirates
http://www.emirates.com/

Gulf air
http://www.gulfairco.com/

Japan Airlines
http://www.jal.co.jp/e/index.html

KLM Royal Dutch Airlines
http://www.klm.nl/

Korean Air
http://www.koreanair.com/

Kuwait Airways
http://www.travelfirst.com/sub/kuwaitair.html

Lufthansa German Airline
http://www.lufthansa.com/

Malaysia Airlines
http://www.malaysiaairlines.com.my/

North West Airlines

http://www.nwa.com/

Qantas Airways Ltd

http://www.qantas.com/

Qatar Airways Ltd.

http://qatarairways.com/

Royal Jordanian

http://www.rja.com.jo/

Saudi Arabia Airlines

http://www.saudiairlines.com/

Scandinavian Airlines Syatem

http://www.flysas.com/

Singapore Airlines

http://www.singaporeair.com/

South African Airways

http://www.flysaa.com/

Swiss Air

http://www.swissair.com/

Tarom Romania Air Transport

http://tarom.digiro.net/

Thai Airways International

http://www.thaiair.com/

United Airlines

http://www.ual.com/

Yemen Airways

http://home.earthlink.net/~yemenair/

China Airlines

http://www.china-airlines.com/us/index.htm

Railways

Online Rail Reservation

http://irctc.co.in/

Indian Railways

http://www.indianrail.gov.in/

State Tourism

Andaman and Nicobar Islands

http://andaman.nic.in/

AP Tourism

http://www.aptourism.com/
http://www.andhrapradesh.com/
http://www.apinfrastructure.com/

Arunachal Pradesh

http://www.arunachaltourism.com/
http://arunachalpradesh.nic.in/

Assam

http://assamgovt.nic.in/

Bihar

http://bihar.nic.in/

http://www.nic.in/ptdc/

Chhattisgarh

http://cgtourism.nic.in/

New Delhi

http://www.newdelhi.net/defaultr.htm

Kerala Tourism

http://www.keralatourism.org/

Goa

http://www.goacom.com/
http://goagovt.nic.in/
http://goatourism.nic.in/
http://www.goatrip.com/
http://www.goahub.com/goa/travel_guide
http://ruralbazargoa.nic.in/
http://goamuseum.nic.in/

Gujarat

http://www.gujarattourism.com/

Haryana

http://www.nic.in/htc/

Himachal Pradesh

http://www.hptdc.nic.in/

Karnataka

http://kstdc.nic.in/
http://www.karnatakatourism.com/

Kerala Tourism

http://www.keralatourism.org/

Madhya Pradesh Tourism

http://www.mptourism.com/

Maharashtra

http://www.maharashtra.gov.in/

http://www.mumbainet.com/

Manipur

http://manipur.nic.in/

Meghalaya

http://meghalaya.nic.in/
http://www.meghalayatourism.com/

Orissa

http://www.orissa-tourism.com/

Pondicherry

http://www.tourisminpondicherry.com/

Punjab

http://www.nic.in/ptdc/
punjabgovt.nic.in/page2

chandigarh.nic.in

Rajasthan

http://www.rajgovt.org/
http://www.rajasthantourism.gov.in/

Sikkim

http://sikkim.nic.in/
http://www.sikkimtourism.org/

Tamil Nadu

http://www.tamilnadutourism.org//
http://www.tidco.com/

Tripura

http://tripura.nic.in/

Uttar Pradesh

http://www.up-tourism.com/

Others

Department of Development of North Eastern Region
http://www.northeast.nic.in/

Cottage Industry

http://www.cottageemporiumindia.com/

WTI (World Travel India)

http://www.worldtravelindia.com/

SATTE

http://www.satte.org/

SOUKYA - The International Holistic Healt
Centre

http://www.soukya.com/

APPENDIX—III

PROGRAMME OF WORLD SUMMIT ON SUSTAINABLE DEVELOPMENT, 2002

Johannesburg, South Africa: 26 August-4 September 2002

EVENTS

Monday, 2 September 2002

Side Events

1.15 p.m.- 2.45 p.m.	African Coastal Management, organized by the Government of South Africa (Ballroom 1)
1.15 p.m. - 2.45 p.m.	East-West Environmental Partnership for Sustainable Development, organized by the Governments of Ukraine, Georgia, the Netherlands and Denmark (Committee Room 4 (a))
6.30 p.m. - 8 p.m.	The Social Dimension of Globalization: a Dialogue with Civil Society, organized by the World Commission on the Social Dimension of Globalization (Ballroom 1)
6.30 p.m. - 8 p.m.	The Sino-Italian Cooperation Program for Environmental Protection Towards Sustainable Development: an Example of Partnership, organized by the Governments of Italy and China (Committee Room 4 (a))

Programme of Meetings

Please check the programme of meetings published in the *Journal* against the scrolling screens.

Note: The programme of meetings, agenda and events and the summary of the meetings of the Summit appear in the main part of the *Journal* (No. 9).

Major Groups and NGOs Caucus Meetings

Monday, 2 September 2002

8 a.m. -8:45 a.m.	Ecumenical Team (Major Groups Room, Plenary Section)
8.45 a.m.-10 a.m.	Sustainable Development Issues Network (Major Groups Room, Plenary Section)
10a.m.-11 a.m.	Women (Major Groups Room, Plenary Section) Sustainable Production and Consumption Patterns (Major Groups Room, Caucus Room A)
11 a.m.-12 noon	Youth (Major Groups Room, Plenary Section)
	Peace (Major Groups Room, Caucus Room A)
12 noon -1 p.m.	Sustainable Agriculture and Food Systems ((Major Groups Room, Plenary Section)
	Fresh Water (Major Groups Room, Caucus Room A)
1 p.m. -2 p.m.	Southern NGOs (Major Groups Room, Plenary Section) Human

	Rights, Environment and Development (Major Groups Room, Caucus Room A)
3 p.m.-4 p.m.	Health (Major Groups Room, Caucus Room A)
4 p.m. -5 p.m.	Energy and Climate (Major Groups Room, Plenary Section) Cultural Diversity (Major Groups Room, Caucus Room A)
5 p.m.-6 p.m.	Indigenous Peoples (Major Groups Room, Plenary Section)

Press Conferences

Press conferences will be held in the Press Conference Room (level -2) and will be open to representatives of accredited press only.

Monday, 2 September 2002

10 a.m.	H.E. Mr. Anders Fogh Rasmussen, Prime Minister of Denmark and President of the European Union
	H.E. Mr. Romano Prodi, President of the European Commission
11.30 a.m.	Five Children Speaking at the Plenary
12 noon	Daily press briefing by Ms. Susan Mark-ham, Spokeswoman for the Summit, and Mr. Lowell Flanders, Senior United Nations Adviser Coordinating the Drafting Groups
12.30 p.m.	Daily press briefing by the

	Spokesman for the Host Government
1.30 p.m.	H.E. Mr. Jacques Chirac, President of France
	H.E. Mr. Tony Blair, Prime Minister of the United Kingdom
2.30 p.m.	Caribbean Governments - Global Sustainable Energy Islands Initiative
3 p.m.	Abu Dhabi Global Environmental Data Initiative (AGEDI): H.H. Sheikh Hamad Bin Mohamed Al Sharqi, Head of the United Arab Emirates (UAE) Delegation to WSSD, Ruler of Fujairah, United Arab Emirates
3.30 p.m.	Initiative to Grow Sustainable Business in World's Poorest Countries
6.30 p.m.	International Law for Sustainable Development

Announcements

WORLD SUMMIT ON SUSTAINABLE DEVELOPMENT

Johannesburg, South Africa (26 August-4 September 2002)

General Debate (2-4 September)

The provisional list of speakers (No. 5) for the general

debate to be held from 2 to 4 September 2002 will be available *today,* 30 August 2002, *at noon* in Boardroom 2. The provisional list and updated versions will also be posted on the website of the Summit at www.johannesburgsummit.org. Participants are reminded that the time-limit set for statements in the general debate is 5 minutes. Delegations who have not yet done so are requested to communicate the name and title of their speaker to the secretariat in writing (Ms. June Chesney: Boardroom 2; tel.: (11) 508-0339; fax : (11) 508-0933; email: chesney@un.org).

Round Tables (2-4 September)

In accordance with decision 2002/PC/6 of its preparatory committee, the Summit will organize four round tables in parallel with the general debate on Monday, 2 September, at 3 p.m., Tuesday, 3 September, at 10 a.m. and 3 p.m. and Wednesday, 4 September, at 10 a.m.

Each round table will comprise up to 50 seats for Government delegations who will be inscribed on a first-come first-served basis, with due regard to level of participation. Delegations are reminded that they may participate in only one round table discussion. States wishing to participate in the round tables are invited to inscribe with the secretariat (Ms. Nancy Beteta: Boardroom 4; tel.: (11) 508-0283; fax: (11) 508-1584; email: beteta@un.org).

General Statements (29 and 30 August)

In accordance with decision 2002/PC/6 of the preparatory committee for the Summit, general statements by entities, intergovernmental organizations and other entities that have received a standing invitation from the United Nations General Assembly to participate in their capacity of observers in the sessions and work of all international conferences convened under its auspices, by the specialized agencies and other intergovernmental organizations, interested United Nations organs, and by the associate members of the regional commissions, will be made in the plenary in the afternoon and evening of 29 August and in the morning, afternoon and evening of 30 August 2002. Participants are reminded that the time-limit set for general statements is 5 minutes. The list of speakers in this regard is now open and communications should be sent to the secretariat in writing (Ms. Isabelle Martinez: Boardroom 2; tel.: (11) 508-0796; fax: (11) 508-0933: email: martinez9@un.org).

Announcement

PROTOCOL ARRANGEMENTS FOR THE HIGH LEVEL SEGMENT OF THE WORLD SUMMIT ON SUSTAINABLE DEVELOPMENT (2-4 SEPTEMBER)

Welcoming Reception

Today, 2 September, in the morning, the President of South Africa, the United Nations Secretary-General and their spouses will co-host a welcoming reception at the Sandton Convention Centre on the fourth floor VIP Lounge in honour of Heads of State/Heads of Government, Vice-Presidents and Crown Princes (HS/HG/VP/CP) and their spouses from 7.30 a.m. to 8.50 a.m. After the reception, HS/HG/VP/CP and their spouses will be escorted to the fifth floor where the Military Liaison Officers will escort them to their seats. The VIP lounge on the fourth floor will be reserved exclusively for the use of the VVIPs throughout the high level segment of the summit.

Arrival

The dignitaries will begin arriving at the Sandton

Convention Centre at 7.30 a.m. where they will be greeted and escorted by Protocol. For each delegation led by HS/HG/VP/CP (VVIP) a motorcade consisting of four vehicles will come to the Centre at two drop off points namely the tented south side main entrance and the garage south entrance. Upon arrival at the tented south side main entrance, only the VVIP and spouse will disembark the vehicle. The rest of the delegation will be dropped off at the tented north side entrance and take the elevators or escalators to their destinations. The motorcade arriving at the south side elevators in the garage will discharge the VVIP and spouse and the rest of the delegation will be dropped off at the north elevators in the garage to proceed to their destinations.

The VVIPs and spouses who stay in Michelangelo will walk to the Centre between 8 a.m. and 8.10 a.m. The VVIPs coming by foot from the Sandton Sun Intercontinental and Sandton Towers to the Centre will use the Skywalk from 8.10 a.m. to 8.20 a.m.

Access Cards to the Sandton Convention Centre

Due to the tremendous concern over safety and security problems related to overcrowding in the building, it has become necessary to take additional measures to restrict the number of persons entering the Sandton Convention Centre starting *today,* 2 September.

Delegations are advised that in addition to the primary SCC passes, each delegation of Member States will be issued up to twenty access cards to the Sandton Convention Centre. It is important to note that this card will give access to the SCC, but the movements inside the Center will be further regulated by the following:

All the delegations of Member States will be issued four cards in accordance with the number of seats at the delegation tables in the plenary hall. In addition, each delegation of Member States will be issued two access cards for the designated overflow area in the back of the plenary hall.

As regards observer delegations of Inter-governmental Organizations, United Nations Specialized Agencies, and Associate Members of the United Nations Regional Economic Commissions, they will be issued up to ten access cards to the Sandton Convention Centre plus two additional cards to the plenary hall in accordance with the number of seats allocated to them at the delegation tables.

All the abovementioned cards can be picked up by authorized representatives of delegations at the accreditation center as of 29 August 2002.

Plenary Meeting

During the Plenary meetings all HS/HG/VP/CP will be escorted from their delegation seats approximately five minutes before their statements to the podium and escorted back to their seats after their statements. All delegations represented at this level are requested to ensure that their heads of delegations are at their seats at least ten minutes prior to their statements.

South African Events

An Official Banquet will be hosted by President T M Mbeki and Mrs. Z M Mbeki for Heads of State, Heads of Government, Royalty and spouses at Maroela Room, Sandton Sun Towers Hotel, Sandton today, 2 September. The arrival of invitees is expected between 7.30 p.m. and 8 p.m.

A Banquet for Heads of Delegation (Ministerial) will

be hosted by the Premier Gauteng, Mr. S. Shilowa and the Mayor of the City of Johannesburg, Mr. A. Masondo at Civic Theatre, Braamfontein on 3 September. The arrival of invitees is expected between 6.30 p.m. and 7 p.m.

Invitations to both events will be handed over by Military Liaison Officers.

GENERAL INFORMATION

Circulation of Statements

A minimum of 35 copies of the text of speeches to be delivered in plenary and other meetings should be given in advance to the conference officer. If general distribution is required, 450 copies are necessary. Statements for the plenary on Monday morning should be delivered between 8 a.m. and 9.30 a.m.

Requests for Meeting Services

Requests for meeting services should be directed to Ms. Gail Grossman, Chief of Meetings Services (Boardroom 6) (tel.: 508-0885; cellular phone: 0832962055).

Circulation of Written Statements

Though there is no general debate during the ministerial segment, if delegations wish to have written statements distributed to all delegations, observers, specialized agencies and press officers, 350 copies are required. Participants in the session are reminded that the Secretariat will not be in a position to offer reproduction services for such texts.

Delegations who wish to have written statements distributed to the media are requested to deliver 350 copies to the media documents counter located in the Media Centre on the exhibition level (basement) of the Sandton Convention Centre.

Delegations who wish to have their statements posted on the Internet are requested to send an advance electronic copy of their statements, in any of the official languages, to the Media Centre or to the following e-mail address: webcast @un.org.

Request for Bilateral Meetings During the Summit (2-4 September 2002)

To book a bilateral room, please contact Esperanza Suarez-Anaya at the Sandton Convention Center (tel.: 011-508-0884, fax: 011-5081584, or email: suareze@un.org).

Requests for Press Conferences

To book a press conference, please contact Maricel Ma-gas-Sniffen at the Sandton Convention Centre (tel.: 011-508-0374, fax 011-508-1248, or e-mail magas-sniffen@un.org).

Media Contacts

To facilitate media contact, delegations are invited to provide the Office of the Spokeswoman with the name and telephone number in Johannesburg of the person in the delegation who journalists may contact to request interviews or other information. Please contact Pragati Pascale (tel.: 011-508-0923, or cellular phone: 083-296-2393).

Internet Coverage

The Department of Public Information will provide Internet coverage of the session. Internet users around the world will be able to follow the proceedings of the session by viewing the live webcast and accessing information such as press releases, daily highlights, official documents, daily journal, statements and other information material at the following URL:

Arabic: www.un.org/arabic/conferences/wssd/

Chinese: www.un.org/chinese/events/wssd/

English: www.johannesburgsummit.org/

French: www.un.org/french events/wssd/

Russian: www.un.org/russian/conferen/wssd/

Spanish: www.un.org/spanish/conferences/wssd/

Information on Partnerships Launched During Side Events or Parallel Events

Information on those partnerships which have not yet been submitted to the Summit Secretariat, but will be launched during side events or parallel events, should be provided to the Summi Secretariat as soon as possible.

The following information is required in order to include those partnerships in a Conference Room paper summarizing Parterships for the World Summit on Social Development; geographical coverage, partners, contact information, financial commitments, objectives and concrete targets. Please contact Ms. Monika Linn (tel.: 508 2048, e-mail: linnm@un.org). I f you wish your partnership to be posted to the official United Nations Web site (www.johannesburgsummit.org),please fill in the table available on thw Web site and forward it to Ms. Monika Linn via e-mail (linnm@un.org).

APPENDIX—IV

THE MUNICIPAL SOLID WASTES

THE MUNICIPAL SOLID WASTES (MANAGEMENT AND HANDLING) RULES, 2000

Central Government notified in exercise of the Powers conferred by Section 3, 6 and 25 of the Environment (Protection) Act, 1986 with the objective of regulating the management and handling of the Municipal Solid Wastes.

Applicability

Apply to all municipal authorities responsible for collection, segregation, storage, transportation processing and disposal of municipal solid wastes.

Responsibility of Municipal Authority

1. Every municipal authority shall, within the territorial area of the municipality, be responsible for the implementation of the provisions of these rules, and for any infrastructure development for collection, storage, segregation, transportation, processing and disposal of municipal solid wastes.
2. The municipal authority or an operator of a facility shall make an application in Form-I, for grant of authorisation for setting up waste processing and disposal facility including landfills from the State Board or the Committee in order to comply with the implementation programme laid down in Schedule-I.
3. The municipal authority shall comply with these rules as per the implementation schedule laid down in Schedule-I.

4. The municipal authority shall furnish its annual report in Form-II.

   (a) to the Secretary-incharge of the Department of Urban Development of the concerned State or as the case may be of the Union Territory, in case of a metropolitan city; or

   (b) to the District Magistrate or the Deputy Commissioner concerned in case of all other town and cities, with a copy to the State Board or the Committee on or before the 30th day of June every year.

Management of Municipal Solid Wastes

(1) Any municipal solid waste generated in a city or a town, shall be managed and handled in accordance with the compliance criteria and the procedure laid down in Schedule-II

(2) The waste processing and disposal facilities to be set up by the municipal authority on their own or through an operator of a facility shall meet the specifications and standards as specified in Schedule-III and Schedule-IV.

APPENDIX—VI

THE NOISE POLLUTION (REGULATION AND CONTROL) RULES, 2000

Introduction

Whereas the increasing ambient noise levels in public places from various sources, inter-alia, industrial activity, construction activity, generator sets, loud speakers, public address systems, music systems, vehicular horns and other mechanical devices have deleterious effects on human health and the psychological well being of the people, it is considered necessary to regulate and control noise producing and generating sources with the objective of maintaining the ambient air quality standards in respect of noise;

Whereas a draft of Noise Pollution (Control and Regulation) Rules, 1999 was published under the notification of the Government of India in the Ministry of Environment and Forests vide number S.O. 528 (E) dated the 2e June, 1999 inviting objections and suggestions from all the persons likely to be affected thereby, before the expiry of the period of sixty days from the date on which the copies of the Gazette containing the said notification are made available to the public-,

And whereas copies of the said Gazette were made available to the public on the I" day of July, 1999.

And whereas the objections and suggestions received from the public in respect of the said draft rules have been duly considered by the Central Government-,

Now, therefore, in exercise of the powers conferred by clause (ii) of sub-section (2) of section 3, sub-section (1) and clause (b) of sub-section (2) of section 6 and section 25 of the Environment (Protection) Act, 1986 (29 of 1986) read with rule 5 of the Environment (Protection) Rules, 1986, the Central Government hereby makes the following rules for the regulation and control of noise producing and generating sources, namely:

The Noise Pollution (Regulation and Control) Rules, 2000

1. *Short-Title and Commencement*

(1) These rules may be called the-Noise Pollution (Regulation and Control) Rules, 2000.

(2) They shall come into force on the date of their publication in the Official Gazette.

2. *Definitions*

In these rules, unless the context otherwise requires,

(a) "Act" means the Environment (Protection) Act, 1986 (29 of 1986);

(b) "area/zone" means all areas which fall in either of the four categories given in the Schedule annexed to these rules;

(c) "authority" means any authority or officer authorised by the Central Government, or as the case may be, the State Government in accordance with the laws in force and includes a District Magistrate, Police Commissioner, or any other officer designated for the maintenance of the ambient air quality standards in respect of noise under any law for the time being in force;

(d) "person" in relation to any factory or premises means a person or occupier or his agent, who has control over the affairs of the factory or premises;

(e) "State Government" in relation to a Union territory means the Administrator thereof appointed under article 239 of the Constitution.

[It is hoped that the text of various statutes reproduced in the preceding pages will enlighten the readers, who are more akin to side-effects of mega international events/

Bibliography

Adham Khan's Tomb *The Delhi that No-one Knows*, by R.V. Smith. Orient Longman, 2005.

Aitken, Bill (2001). *Speaking Stones: World Cultural Heritage Sites in India*. Eicher Goodearth Limited.

Alfred Frederick; Pollock Harcourt. *The New Guide to Delhi*. PaperbackshopUS.

Annon. All About Delhi *Delhi, the Capital of India*, by Anon. Asian Educational Services, 1997.

Annon (1997). *Dictionary of Islamic architecture: Delhi, the capital of India*. Asian Educational Services. p. 55–56.

Annual York-Noor Lecture Series: "Murder, Mausolea and the Emperor Akbar: Two Early Mughal Tombs" *York University*.

Anthony Welch. "A Medieveal Centre of Learning in India: The Hauz Khas Madrasa in Delhi -application" (pdf).

Arundhati Basu (2004-06-26). "Wisps of the past through Dilli's golden gates". *The Times of India*.

Asher, Catherine B. (2000). "Delhi walled: Changing Boundaries". in James D. Tracy. *City Walls*. Cambridge University Press. pp. 247–281.

Asher, Catherine B. Adham Khan's Tomb - Image and History, *The New Cambridge History of India*, Cambridge University Press.

ASI have included the remaining unprotected monuments of Lodhi Garden under the Delhi Circle protection umbrella *The Hindu*, October 16, 2002.

Austin, Ian; Thhakur Nahar Singh Jasol. "Chauhans (Cahamanas, Cauhans)". *The Mewar Encyclopedia.*

Bakshi, S.R. (1995). *Delhi Through Ages*. Anmol Publications Pvt. Ltd. p. 2.

Batra, N. L. (1996). *Heritage conservation: preservation and restoration of monuments*. Aryan Books International.

Beyond the WALL *The Hindu*, September 25, 2003.

Chandra, Satish (2003). *History of architecture and ancient building materials in India*. Tech Books International.

Cohen, Richard J. (October–December 1989). "An Early Attestation of the Toponym Dhilli". *Journal of the American Oriental Society* 109 (4): 513–519.

Delhi city guide, by Eicher Goodearth Limited, Delhi Tourism. Published by Eicher Goodearth Limited, 1998.

Dr. Akbar Ahmed. "The Trial of Dara Shikoh:A Play in Three Acts" (pdf). The Buxton Readings. p. 53.

Eicher:City Guide - Delhi, Eicher Goodearth Publication. 1998. ISBN 8190060120. *Page 117*

Fanshawe.H.C (1998). *Delhi, Past and Present*. Asian Educational Services. pp. 1 to 8.

Fatehpuri Shahi Masjid: A mute witness to the travails of Dillee milligazette. May 1, 2000.

Geraldine Forbes; Gordon Johnson, B. R. Tomlinson, Stewart Gordon, and Catherine Ella Blanshard Asher (1992). *The new Cambridge history of India*. Cambridge University Press. p. 10.

Gordon Sanderson; Maulvi Shuaib (2000). *Delhi Fort*. Asia Publication Services. pp. 80,81 & 82.

Hedger-Gourlay, Fiona coauthors = Lindy Ingham, Jo Newton, Emma Tabor and Jill Worrell (2006-09-13). "Lal Kot and Siri" (pdf).

Javeed, Tabassum (2008). *World Heritage Monuments and Related Edifices in India*. Algora Publishing. p. 107.

Kevin R. D. Shepherd. *A Sufi matriarch: Hazrat Babajaný*. Anthropographia Publications.

Lucy Peck (2005). *Delhi - A thousand years of Building*. New Delhi: Roli Books Pvt Ltd.. pp. 135, 181, & 241.

M H Syed (2004). *History of Delhi Sultanate*. Anmol Publications Pvt. Ltd.. p. 413.

Madan Mohan. "Historical Information System for Surveying Monuments and Spatial Data Modeling for Conservation of Cultural Heritage in Delhi" (pdf). pp. 5/16 & 5/17.

Mahtab Jahan (2004). "Dilli's gates and windows". MG The Milli Gazette Indian Muslims leading new paper.

Mayaram, Shail. *Against history, against state: counterperspectives from the margins*, Cultures of history. Columbia University Press, 2003.

Mohan, I.(1992). *The world of walled cities: conservation, environmental pollution, urban renewal and developmental prospects*. Mittal Publications. p. 23.

Mountstuart Elphinstone; Edward Byles Cowell (2006-06-27). *The History of India: The Hindú and Mahometan Periods*. Scientific Society (Aligarh, India),

Mukherjee, Soma. Royal Mughal Ladies and Their Contributions, Gyan Books, 2001.

Nath, R. (1978). *History of Sultanate architecture*. Abhinav Publications. p. 22.

Necipoglu, Gulru (2002). "Epigraphs, Scripture, and Architecture in the Early Sultanate of Delhi". *Muqarnas: An Annual on the Visual Culture of the Islamic World.* BRILL. pp. 12–43.

Page, J.A. (1926) "An Historical Memoir on the Qutb, Delhi" *Memoirs of the Archaeological Society of India* 22: OCLC 5433409; republished (1970) Lakshmi Book Store, New Delhi.

Patrick Horton; , Richard Plunkett and Hugh Finlay (2002). *Delhi*. Lonely Planet. p. 232.

Patrick Horton; Richard Plunkett and Hugh Fnlay (2002). *Delhi*. Lonely Planet. pp. 92–94.

Peck (2005). *Delhi - A thousand years of Building*. New Delhi: Roli Books Pvt Ltd..

Petersen. Andrew . Mughals *Dictionary of Islamic architecture*, Routledge, 1996.

Poonam Bisht (2005-12-07). "A serious blow to Delhi's heritage as Army plans to build residential complex close to Sultan Garhi". Delhi Scoop.

Schimmel, Annemarie; Burzine K. Waghmar (2004). *The Empire of the great Mughals*. Reaktion Books, p. 267.

Sehgal, R.L. (1998) [1998]. *Slum Upgradation: Emerging Issue & Policy Implication's*. Bookwell Publications.

Sharma, Y.D. (2001). *Delhi and its Neighbourhood*. New Delhi: Archeological Survey of India. pp. 22, 83–84.

Shiri Ram Bakshi (1995). *Delhi Through Ages*. Anmol Publications Pvt. Ltd.

Smith, George (1882). *The Geography of British India, Political & Physical*. J. Murray.

Tyagi, Pankaj. "Country's first tomb is victim of ASI's

neglect". The Indian Muslim's Leading News Paper Milli Gazette.

Upadhyay, R (16 February 2004). *Sufism in India: Its Origin, History and Politics*.. South Asia Analysis Group.

World Heritage Sites - Humayun's Tomb: Characteristics of Indo-Islamic architecture, Archaeological Survey of India (ASI).

Index

■■■